"My friend Dan Kennedy is unique, a genius in many ways. I have always admired his ability to see the vital truths in any business and to state these realities with straight language and clear definitions. His approach is direct. His ideas are controversial. His ability to get results for his clients is unchallenged."

—Brian Tracy, from his introduction to Dan's *No B.S. Business Success* book

(Brian Tracy is one of America's most sought after speakers and the author of dozens of business books. www.BrianTracy.com)

"Dan has literally eliminated the B.S. in explaining great ways to make more sales."

—Tom Hopkins, from his introduction to Dan's *No B.S. Sales Success* book

(Tom Hopkins is world-renowned as a master sales trainer. www.TomHopkins.com)

"My restaurant grossed over $6 million every year I owned it.
But to back up, to 'Before Dan Kennedy', I was a persistent
salesperson and I loved it. I did well as a single female in
the auto industry, in 1985, right out of college, I was
making over $40,000.00 a year. In 1993, I married and
with my husband, started two profitable businesses:
a fire and water restoration business, and a
construction company. In 2000, I was approached by a
restaurant owner who wanted to open a second Japanese
steakhouse. Ultimately, we ended the other businesses and
focused on the restaurant. **It was Kennedy-style marketing
that fueled an exceptional restaurant business.** We received
64 People's Choice awards, I gathered **over 63,000 customers,**
I had 6 to 14 different promotions going on *simultaneously**
each month (*a Renegade Millionaire lesson I learned from
Dan), we grossed over $6.5 million a year with about
$1 million in profits. An independent restaurant valuation
firm analyzing the business for its sale said that, quote,
less than 5% of the 945,000 food service establishments
in the U.S. employ the advanced techniques and get
the outstanding results Nakama has enjoyed as a
direct result of its marketing. They stated that my
restaurant was three times more successful than
comparable restaurants because of my marketing.
Ultimately, I sold the business. I'm beginning
a new journey as an entrepreneur and a coach.

—Becky Auer, www.profitcatapultbusinessschool.com

THE

NO B.S.

GUIDE TO

DIRECT
MARKETING

SECOND EDITION

BY

DAN S. KENNEDY

WITH SPECIAL GUEST CHAPTERS FROM

BEN GLASS AND CRAIG PROCTOR
AND SPECIAL INTERVIEW WITH
RICHARD SEPPALA

EP

**Entrepreneur
PRESS®**

Publisher: Entrepreneur Press
Cover Design: Andrew Welyczko
Production and Composition: Eliot House Productions

This publication is designed to provide accurate and authoritative information in regard to the subject matter covered. It is sold with the understanding that the publisher is not engaged in rendering legal, accounting, or other professional services. If legal advice or other expert assistance is required, the services of a competent professional person should be sought.

Library of Congress Cataloging-in-Publication Data
Kennedy, Dan S., 1954–
    No B.S. direct marketing : the ultimate no holds barred, kick butt, take no prisoners direct marketing for non-direct marketing businesses/by Dan S. Kennedy.—Second Edition.
    p.   cm.
    ISBN-13: 978-1-59918-501-9 (alk. paper)
    ISBN-10: 1-59918-501-6 (alk. paper)
    1. Direct marketing. I. Title.
    HF5415.126.K46 2013
    658.8'72—dc23   2012043709

Printed in the United States of America

17 16 15   10 9 8 7 6 5

Contents

SECTION II

APPLICATION

SECTION III

RESOURCES

The End of Advertising and Marketing As *You* Know It

In the first edition of this book, back in 2006, before the recession, before the explosion of social media and the importance given it as a marketing media, before all sorts of new media demanding business owners' attention, I wrote: Most small-business advertising and marketing stinks. I said: Monstrous sums are wasted, and opportunities lost. In the ensuing years, there's been a whole lot of change. But this hasn't, at least not for the better. Today, businesspeople are really, really, really confused and overwhelmed and hollered at; told that they *must* do this, that, the other thing, more and more—just to get the same results. Or less. I am here to mute the noise. To guide you to clarity, about a relatively short list of fundamental principles and strategies that can prevent your being lost in a deep, dense forest of media demanding your attention, time, and money.

We can begin with the radical, challenging idea that just about everything you see big business doing is wrong for you—if you run a small business, a private practice, a service enterprise, or even a midsize, growth company. Big companies have different objectives, agendas, constituencies to satisfy, CEO egos to salve as well as different resources and depth of resources than you do. If you study them at all, you must time-travel to examine what they did in journey from start to small and ultimately to big, not what they do now. If the rabbit emulates the lion, and sits on a rock, doesn't move, and roars loud and often, all the rabbit accomplishes is making it easier for predators to find him and eat him.

It's also worth noting that, very often, the bigger a company grows, the dumber it gets. This is the result of having more and more people in it spending somebody's money other than their own and being safely distanced by bureaucracy from direct and immediate financial consequences of their decisions and from where rubber meets road, on the store or showroom floor, face to face with customers, clients, or patients. These people are insulated from reality and very vulnerable to charlatanism prevalent inside ad agencies, social media agencies, and other shovel sellers. In the great Gold Rush, more money was made by the sellers of shovels—mules, mining equipment and tools, and maps— than by those actually searching for the gold. It's dressed up differently today, but the truth is unchanged.

The fact is that most of your peers are blind mice leading other blind mice. The proof is in the financial facts of every category of business, every profession, every sales organization, every population: 1% create tremendous incomes and wealth,

4% do very well, 15% earn good livings, 60% stall, stagnate, struggle endlessly, and 20% fail. Working back up, you have an 80% poor/20% prosperous ratio, a 95% v. 5%, even a 99% v. 1% ratio. Thus, the overwhelming majority of your peers are engaged in marketing that fails them, intellectually and emotionally committed to that failed and failing marketing, and bloated with opinions about why you should follow the same path to frustration and failure. If you refuse, deviate,

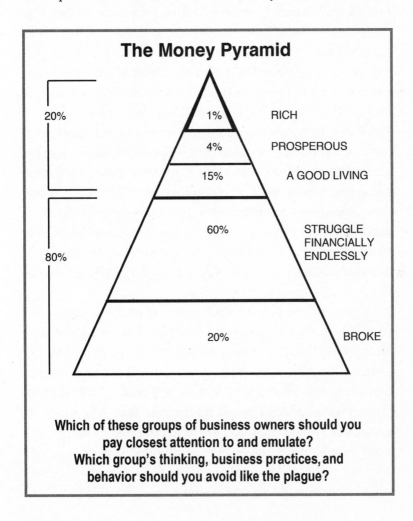

The Money Pyramid

20%

1%   RICH

4%   PROSPEROUS

15%   A GOOD LIVING

80%

60%   STRUGGLE FINANCIALLY ENDLESSLY

20%   BROKE

**Which of these groups of business owners should you pay closest attention to and emulate?
Which group's thinking, business practices, and behavior should you avoid like the plague?**

or even dare to question the validity of this path, your peers and friends and sometimes employees react violently. They mock, they criticize, they shame, they shun. It's important to remember that every critic has his own agenda, whether conscious or subconscious.

Crossing The Great Divide

Next, I offer the even more radical and challenging idea that pretty much everything you think you know and have been conditioned to believe about marketing is wrong. Here, I am going to expose The Great Divide. On one side is the majority of companies and business owners who are married to very traditional, mainstream, brand and name visibility driven, largely unaccountable advertising and marketing. Most of the money invested in it is based on faith and hope. Many people think, falsely, that by using new media they are doing a new kind of marketing. In truth, they merely move the same bad advertising and flawed marketing from one place to another. On the other side is a smaller rag-tag band of rebels and rogues and renegades who utilize *Direct* Marketing. This book will expose The Great Divide between the two.

If you get it, you'll smack yourself in the head for not seeing it all sooner, on your own. You'll be in awe of how much sense it makes. You'll never look at an ad, sales letter, website, etc., the same way again. You'll be ruined toward traditional advertising for life. You will make major changes in your own advertising and marketing—fast. When you do, you *will* be argued with, ridiculed and criticized by employees, peers, competitors, maybe even family and friends. You will need depth of understanding about Direct Marketing to stay strong. The astounding results you'll see from full conversion from Ordinary Marketing to Direct Marketing will convince you, but know you will need courage and discipline to stay your new course. I promise you that being thought a fool or misguided renegade and having millions of dollars trumps being thought of as "normal" and "correct" and "proper" and barely making a living.

I get nearly obscene amounts of money to advise entrepreneurs exclusively on Direct Marketing, and to craft sales copy and marketing systems for them. My current fees begin at $18,800.00 for consulting days, project fees range upwards from $100,000.00 to $1 million plus royalties, and over 85% of all clients stay with me for years. My fees have more than doubled over the past five years. I am busier than I wish to be. I tell you this not to brag, but to impress on you the extremely high value of the information in this book. Nothing, and I mean NOTHING can have as positive and dramatic an impact on your prosperity as crossing The Great Divide to being a Direct Marketer—regardless of your particular products or services, other deliverables, and size of business. This book is not about doing *better* marketing. It is about a total conversion to entirely *different* marketing.

You will get "THE RULES" from me. All my life I've been a rule breaker, so laying down these Rules is a bit odd. But when all this is new, it's best to have strict and rigid and relatively simple Rules and to adhere to them. With depth of understanding, successful experience, and ability, you can later inject creativity and innovation and develop a system uniquely your own. For now, my Rules will rule. You will also meet two terrific practitioners of Direct Marketing in Non-Direct Marketing Businesses: Ben Glass, a lawyer, and Craig Proctor, a real estate agent. And you will see rich examples and be pointed to websites to visit to see even more examples. Out the back of all this, you will be able to transform your business to an infinitely more powerful Direct Marketing business—if you dare.

Book Roadmap

Section I—FOUNDATION

Here is my crash course on Direct Marketing as it can be applied to any business, sales career, or professional practice. Learning or reviewing these fundamentals, and agreeing to The Rules, ready you to create transformational change in your business.

Section II—APPLICATION

In this section, you'll see how Direct Marketing is actually applied by owners of exceptionally successful NON-Direct Marketing businesses, and get "short lists" of application opportunities for a variety of categories of businesses.

Section III—RESOURCES

Here, referrals to websites where you can see full implementation of Direct Marketing in Non-Direct Marketing businesses as well as recommendations for educational resources and tools.

FOUNDATION

CHAPTER 1

The Big Switch

Why Direct Marketing for NON-Direct
Marketing Businesses?

I t is an odd sort of title, isn't it?

If you picked it up hoping for huge breakthroughs in your business, you bought the right book.

But first, I have to get these definitions out of the way.

By non-direct marketing business, I mean anything but a mail-order, catalog, or online marketer who *directly* solicits orders for merchandise.

Examples of direct marketing businesses just about everybody knows are the TV home shopping channels, QVC and HSN, Home Shopping Network; legendary catalogers like Lillian Vernon, J. Peterman, and SkyMall; and contemporary catalog and online catalog/e-commerce companies like Amazon and

Zappos; businesses like Fruit of the Month Club; and mass users of direct mail to sell things like Publishers Clearinghouse.

There are tens of thousands of true direct-marketing businesses. Some are familiar to the general public; many, many more are familiar only to the niche or special interest they serve. For example, I have over 50 direct marketers as clients, each selling books, audio CDs, home study courses, and seminars and services by mail, internet, and print media, and teleseminars, and webinars, which market only to a specific industry or profession—one to carpet cleaners, another to restaurant owners, another to chiropractors, etc. If you are not a chiropractor, you don't know the name Dr. Chris Tomshack and his company Health Source. If you are a chiropractor, it would be hard not to know of him, thanks to his full-page ads in the industry trade journals, massive amounts of direct mail, and other direct marketing. There are also direct marketers unknown by name but known by their products or brands, like a long time client of mine, Guthy-Renker Corporation, the billion-dollar business behind TV infomercials for Pro-Activ acne creams. What all these have in common is their fundamental process of selling direct via media to consumers, with no brick-and-mortar locations or face-to-face contact required.

These are not the folks this book is for, even if they are the kinds of entrepreneurs I work personally with the most.

This book is for the owner of a brick-and-mortar business, a business with a store, showroom or office, a restaurant, a dental practice, an accounting practice, or a funeral home, that is some kind of ordinary business, one most likely local and serving a local market. These are the entrepreneurs who have populated my audiences for two decades, subscribe to my *No B.S. Marketing Letter*, and use my systems to transform those "ordinary" businesses into extraordinary money machines that far, far out perform their industry norms, peers, competitors, and their own wildest imaginations. How do they do it? The big switch is a simple one to state (if more complex to do): they switch from traditional advertising to *direct-response* advertising. They stop emulating ordinary and traditional marketing and instead emulate *direct* marketing.

> Don't wait! Right now go to page 175 and sign up for my special "test drive offer" featuring my "No B.S. Marketing Letter," which includes training webinars that extend and expand on this book.

Most "ordinary" businesses advertise and market like much bigger brand-name companies, so they spend (waste) lots of money on image, brand, and presence. But copycatting these big brand-name companies is like a rabbit behaving like the lion. It makes no sense. The big companies have all sorts of reasons for the way they advertise and market that have nothing to do with getting a customer or making sales! Because your agenda is much simpler, you should find successful businesses with similar agendas to copycat. Those are direct marketers. You and they share the same basic ideas:

1. Spend $1.00 on marketing, get back $2.00 or $20.00, fast, that can be accurately tracked to the $1.00 spent.
2. Do NOT spend $1.00 that does not directly and quickly bring back $2.00 or $20.00.

Please stop and be sure you get this life-changing principle. Be careful who you copy. Be careful who you act

Big Company's Agenda for Advertising and Marketing

1. Please/appease its board of directors (most of whom know zip about advertising and marketing but have lots of opinions)

2. Please/appease its stockholders

3. Look good, look appropriate to Wall Street

4. Look good, appropriate to the media

5. Build brand identity

6. Win awards for advertising

7. Sell something

Your Agenda

1. Sell something. Now.

like. Be careful who you study. If their purpose, objectives, agenda, reasons for doing what they do the way they do it don't match up with your purpose, objectives, agenda, then you should NOT study or emulate or copy them!

Please stop and be sure you get this life-changing corollary principle. Find somebody who is successful, who shares your purpose, objectives, agenda, and pay great attention to what he does and how he does it.

I believe some call this sort of thing "a blinding flash of the obvious." Well, you can call it obvious if you like, but then how do you explain the fact that 99% of all businesspeople are operating as if ignorant of this obvious logic?

I might add, this principle has power in places other than marketing. You *can* eventually get south by going due north, but life's easier and less stressful, and business more profitable, if you actually get headed in the direction that leads to your destination of choice. Emulating inappropriate examples is the equivalent of trudging south to get to the North Pole. Odds are, you'll get lost, tired, or eaten by a giant iguana long before seeing snow.

Why Is There So Much Lousy, Unproductive, Unprofitable Advertising and Marketing Out There, Anyway?

No B.S. truth. Most business owners are just about clueless when it comes to advertising and marketing. They are therefore often Advertising Victims, preyed on by media salespeople and ad agencies and others who don't know any more about how to actually produce a customer or make a sale than they do! If you try to get a business owner to accurately tell you where his customers and sales come from, what it costs to get a customer from source A or source B, what results specifically come from this ad or that one, he can't. He's guessing. Consequently, he's often grumpy and unhappy about things he shouldn't be, but also wasting money he needn't be.

The reasons for the cluelessness and vulnerability to victimization are many. Here's a big one: Marketing Incest. When you got into whatever business you're in, you probably looked around at what everybody else in the business was doing and copied it. Gradually, you've tried to do it better, but not radically different, just better. So you have everybody in an industry standing in a circle looking inward at each other, ignoring anyone or anything outside the circle. It's incestuous, and it works just like real generational incest: Everybody slowly gets dumber and dumber and dumber.

All of the people you'll meet in this book did something very different. They turned their back on the circle and deliberately went far afield from their peers in search of different—not just incrementally better, but different—ways of marketing. Now you will, too.

Yes, Salvation Is Within Reach

Now, here's the good news: Most business owners, clueless as they may be about profitable advertising or effective marketing, do know a lot about how to *sell* their products or services. That's very good news because *DIRECT Marketing for NON-*

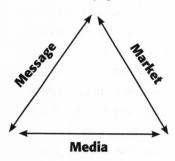

Direct Marketing Businesses is really not about traditional advertising or marketing at all. It is simply "salesmanship multiplied in media." So you actually already do have a firm grip on one-third of the KENNEDY RESULTS TRIANGLE that you'll master with this book. You know the Message. It'll get tweaked, as I'll explain. But you do have this component.

The No B.S. Rules

I'll lay our foundation first. (A radical idea, itself!) Please copy these and post them somewhere you'll see them often until you get them memorized. Doing so will keep you on track, save you a lot of money, and dramatically improve your marketing.

From now on, every ad you run, every flier you distribute, every postcard or letter you mail, every website you put up, every/anything you do MUST adhere to these rules. To be fair, they are simplistic and dogmatic, and there are reasons to violate them in certain situations. But for now, sticking to them as a rigid diet will work. You can experiment later, after you've first cleansed your business of toxins.

Rule #1. There Will Always Be an Offer or Offer(s)

Rule #2. There Will Be a Reason to Respond Right Now

Rule #3. You Will Give Clear Instructions

Rule #4. There Will Be Tracking, Measurement, and Accountability

Rule #5. Only No-Cost Brand-Building

Rule #6. There Will Be Follow-Up

Rule #7. There Will Be Strong Copy

Rule #8. It Will Look Like Mail-Order Advertising

Rule #9. Results Rule. Period.

Rule #10. You Will Be A Tough-Minded Disciplinarian and Put Your Business on a Strict Direct Marketing Diet

---

We'll tackle each Rule in depth, in the next ten chapters.

I once wrote an entire book about breaking rules, and generally speaking, I think rules are for other, ordinary mortals—certainly not for me, and not for you, either, if you are a true entrepreneur. So you'll chafe at rules here just as I would. However, when you are attempting to undo bad habits and replace them with new ones, some hard-and-fast rules are necessary, temporarily. Once you fully understand these and have lived with them for a reasonable length of time, then feel free to experiment if you wish. But get good at coloring inside the lines before ignoring them altogether.

CHAPTER 2

An Offer They Can't Refuse

There is a certain mindset in direct marketing folks. We are very results oriented. We find it difficult to just go out for a drive or to go to the mall just to hang out and browse—we want a definite destination and at least an estimated time of arrival, and we go to the mall to find and buy something. Most direct marketers can't watch a sports telecast unless they've wagered on the game nor play golf or cards or cribbage but for money. In short, we want to KNOW if we have won. We want to KNOW if we have accomplished an aim. While this tendency gets in the way of a friendly family game night, it is extremely useful in avoiding the vagueness that permeates most business owners' marketing activities.

The chief way we avoid vagueness is with the making of offers.

Rule #1
There Will ALWAYS Be an Offer or Offers

A key distinguishing characteristic of Direct Marketing and Direct-Response Advertising from all other marketing and advertising is the presentation of a very specific offer or offers. Ideally, yours is a Godfather's Offer: an offer that the appropriate prospect or customer for you *can't* refuse! We'll get to the architecture of offers in a few minutes, but first the overarching ideas: one, to make your every communication actually ask somebody to do something, and two, to inject new disciplines of selling and accountability into all your communication with prospects, customers, and the marketplace at large.

If you begin paying attention to advertising and marketing, you'll see that most of it merely shows up and talks about the marketers and advertisers, but does not directly offer something specific to be had by immediately and directly responding. A lot of ads and commercials and business cards and brochures now include websites, Facebook sites where you can go like 'em, etc., but present no Godfather Offer as a compelling reason to go there. All this is undisciplined. It is sending money out to play a backyard game with no rules; worse, no scorekeeping, no clear means of judging victory or defeat. A chaotic mess. When you take this undisciplined approach and simply spend and hope and guess, you're at the mercy of opinion about your marketing. Do you like it? Does your mother-in-law like it? Do your customers say nice things about it? Try putting any of that feedback on a bank deposit slip. This all changes with Direct Marketing.

Direct Marketing imposes discipline.

Direct Marketing imposes discipline. That discipline may be as important and beneficial as the benefit of direct response itself. For some mysterious reason, business owners are willing to let advertising and marketing off the hook, but tend to hold everything else accountable for results and return on investment. If they tie up money in certain product inventory, they expect it to sell—or they refuse to restock it. If they employ a sales representative, they expect him to make sales. If they buy a delivery van, they expect it to start and run so it can make deliveries. If they pay a laborer by the hour, they expect him to clock in, be there, and work for the hour. Yet, marketing and media investments made for marketing are permitted to skate. Only Direct Marketing imposes discipline, by always making an offer or offers, so response to those offers can be tracked and measured.

My old speaking colleague, one of the all-time greats, Zig Ziglar, always described salespeople who wimped out at closing sales and directly demanding orders as "professional *visitors*," not professional salespeople. Since you will be doing selling in print, online, with media, you rarely want to let it be a professional visitor on your behalf. Fire all the wimps. Demand real performance. So your task is to incorporate a direct offer each and every time you put out a message, of any kind, by any means.

I mean: of *any* kind. By *any* means. We teach most business owners to use Thanksgiving greeting cards and/or New Year's greeting cards, with past and lost as well as active customers, clients, or patients, and, often, with unconverted leads too. We also teach no greeting card should arrive without being accompanied by an offer. Typically, the offer will be a gift with visit to showroom or store, gift with purchase, gift for referral, etc., placed in a printed piece inside a separate envelope, inside the greeting card itself, to preserve some separation between the thank-you or new-year sentiment and selling. But we are not shy about our purpose in life either, and it is not merely being professional visitors.

In short, you have a fundamental governance decision to make. Will you let yourself be persuaded or bullied into wasting money on marketing that cannot be *directly* held accountable for results and return on investment? Or will you insist on accountability?

Two Types of Offers

There are basically two types of offers. There is an offer requesting purchase. There is also the lead generation offer, asking only for a person to, in effect, raise their hand, to identify and register themselves as having interest in certain subject matter and information or goods or services, and to invite further communication from you. Often, although not always, the lead generation offer is free. There are times and places for both kinds of offers, but no communication should be devoid of some offer.

The Direct Purchase Offer

An online media like Groupon or a hybrid offline + online media like Valpak deliver some of the simplest, most straightforward direct purchase offers—like "Buy One, Get the 2nd One Free"—used by everybody from pizza shops to window replacement companies. I am not a champion of discounting as strategy, and a co-author, Jason Marrs, and I provide much more sophisticated approaches in our book *No B.S. Price Strategy*. But for illustration purposes, this is a direct purchase offer you're very familiar with and may be using now in your business. Another common direct purchase offer, in place of or combined with discounting, is gift with purchase. These were birthed by direct marketers but have migrated to retail, service professions, and B2B, so they are commonplace. They should be and usually are married to a hard deadline. They certainly provide easy opportunity to accurately measure their effectiveness and production, although, out of ignorance or sloth, many business owners fail to measure.

Direct Purchase Offers have several significant disadvantages. First, they tend to sacrifice price integrity and profitability, and if relied on too frequently, train customers to only respond when a "great deal" is offered. Second, they can only be responded to by people ready and able to buy right this minute—they fail to identify people likely to buy in your category in the near future. Third, they can be easily and quickly comparison shopped, especially if you are conveying the offer online. Still, business does revolve around Direct Purchase Offers.

The Lead-Generation Offer

This is a more interesting kind of offer, because it can substantially reduce the waste factor in advertising, convert a sales culture to a marketing culture, and provide opportunity to build trust and create relationship.

You see lead generation done by direct marketers routinely and regularly. You may not have given them much thought, but now you will. They are commonly used by national direct marketers but rarely used by local small businesses—even though the national and local firms may be in the same product or service categories. For example, a company like Premier Bathtubs, which sells walk-in bathtubs that are safer for elderly people, advertises just about everywhere, offering a free information kit with brochures and a DVD. Once somebody raises their hand and registers themselves as interested in making a home's bathroom safe for themselves or an elderly parent, the company has a marketing opportunity. Oddly, you will almost never catch a local remodeling company duplicating this strategy. Instead, they tend to leap to offering an in-home estimate for work to be done. This is often A Bridge Too Far.

The Important Concept of Threshold Resistance

Arnold Taubman, one of America's most successful mall developers, has spoken and written at length about the concept of Threshold Resistance as it applies to entrances to retail stores and window displays of retail stores. I find it applies even more broadly to Direct Marketing. All offers fall somewhere on a continuum between Low Threshold Offer and High Threshold Offer.

Here are examples of offers that would fall to the right of the middle, toward High Threshold:

Chiropractor	Free Exam
Financial Advisor	Free Seminar
Remodeler	Free Estimate
Restaurant	A Meal and an Experience That May Not Prove Pleasurable

These score toward High Threshold because they can be scary and intimidating to the consumer. They require people to put themselves in uncomfortable positions. They require a decision nearly made, to get care, to find an advisor, to get remodeling done. A great many people with evolving interest or interest that can be stimulated will still not be prepared to take this big of a step forward.

Examples of offers that fall at High Threshold are:

Chiropractor	$29 Exam

Financial Advisor   Free Private Appointment

Examples of Low-Threshold Offers

The lowest threshold offer is for free information, to be sent by mail or Federal Express, or accessed online.

Consider a very ordinary business—a funeral home. Most funeral home advertising is very basic: name, location, years in the community, list of services. The only offer is implied: When you need us, we'll bury you. But even a funeral home can create and put forward a low-threshold, information-based, lead-generation offer that begins a relationship, builds trust, and establishes preference in advance of need, like this:

> For a free "Pre-Need Planning Kit" and Audio CD:
> "19 Financial and Estate Planning Tips for
> Responsible Family Leaders," call our free
> recorded message any time at 000-000-0000.
> It will be sent by mail, no cost, no obligation.

The Hybrid Approach

There is no law that says you must choose just one of these approaches.

Most advertising dramatically suppresses possible response by presenting only a single reason for response. Typically, this is a High-Threshold Offer that requires somebody to be 99.9% ready to buy now. Nobody's coming in for a $29.00 exam unless they are 99% ready to put a chiropractic physician to work on their back pain today. But a lot of people suffering with nagging or episodically recurring back pain, who are having evolving thoughts about doing something about it, would respond to a Low-Threshold Offer of information about "True Causes and Best Ways to Relieve Nagging Back Pain—Without Surgery or Drugs." You don't have to be dead or have a dead family member in the parlor to respond to a High + Medium + Low Threshold, i.e., three reasons to respond ad for the funeral parlor. It can present the usual stuff—here we are, here's what we do, if you have an immediate need, call this number any time, 24 hours a day, 7 days a week, and one of our professionals will be immediately available to assist you—but also present the previously shown Low-Threshold Offer, and a Medium-High-Threshold Offer, too, as shown here:

> For a free "Pre-Need Planning Kit" and Audio CD, "19 Financial and Estate Planning Tips for Responsible Family Leaders," call our free recorded message any time at 000-000-0000. It will be sent by mail, no cost, no obligation.

> Tour our new Lakeside Eternal Rest Gardens, get answers to any questions you have about pre-need planning, by appointment, Monday–Saturday. Call William Tourguide at 000-000-0000. Free Thank-You Gift when you visit: complimentary dinner for two at The Golden Corral Steakhouse.

To be clear, what I've introduced you to is:

1. The use of offers
2. The difference between Low to High-Threshold Offers
3. The use of Lead-Generation Offers
4. Single Reason to Respond vs. Multiple Reasons to Respond

Once a business owner understands these things, his objection is often about possible trade down of response. The fear is that somebody who might call or come in or otherwise respond to a High-Threshold Offer and make an immediate purchase will trade down to a Low-Threshold Offer and delay his purchase or be scooped up by a competitor. While this does happen, it usually affects far fewer people than a business owner fears, and the improved total response and value of leads captured for developments more than makes up for what little trade down occurs. After all, the person who fell off a ladder and has to crawl to the phone isn't gong to trade down from making an appointment with the doctor to requesting a free report or DVD delivered days later by mail. The person with a dead body in the parlor is unlikely to trade down from immediate assistance at the funeral parlor to booking a tour next Thursday. In most cases, you can safely add Low-Threshold Offers without significantly compromising response to a High-Threshold Offer designed for the person ready to buy right this minute.

Ultimately, your decisions about the nature of your offer(s), where they fall on the Low- to High-Threshold continuum, whether or not they feature information, whether they are for lead generation or immediate purchase activity or a hybrid of the two are situational. Different media, different markets, different timing will color those decisions. You should realize you have choices and you can make your marketing dollars work harder for you by offering people more than one reason and more than one means of responding to you. But, no matter what you make of these choices each time you must make them in putting forward marketing, your pledge of honor to Rule #1 must be: There will *always* be an offer or offers.

Rule #2
There Will Be Reason to Respond Right Now

Hesitation and procrastination are among the most common of all human behaviors.

If you are a mail-order catalog shopper, you have—more than once—browsed, folded down corners of pages from which you intended to buy items, set the catalogs aside, and never placed the orders. This happens with every marketing media. People watching a TV infomercial almost buy, but put it off, to do the next time they see it, or jot down the 800 number, to do it later, but later never comes. A shopper enters the mall, sees an outfit she likes, but tells herself she'll stop and look at it and probably get it on her way out. By the time she has walked the mall, had lunch, bought other items, and is headed back to the end of the mall she entered at, she is focused on getting to her car and getting home. The dress spotted on arrival is left behind.

We must be sharply, painfully aware of all the potential response lost to such hesitation. The hidden cost and failure in all advertising and marketing is in the almost-persuaded. They were tempted to respond. They nearly responded. They got right up to the edge of response, but then set it aside to take care of later or to mull over or to check out more the next time they were at their computer. When they get to that edge, we must reach across and pull them past it. There must be good reason for them not to stop short or delay or ponder. There must be *urgency*.

At Disney World, at the parks' closing times, they need to get everybody out quickly, for they have much work to do during the night to be clean, fresh, restocked and ready to reopen on time the next morning. If they offered transportation from the parks to the hotels, resorts, and parking lots until everyone was accommodated, people would stroll, loiter, find a bench to sit on until the crowd thinned. But there are posted and announced times for the last bus and the last boat. Thus there is urgency. (Further, they switch from gentle to up-tempo music, dim lights first in the back sections of the park, and have cast members with flashlights waving people along toward the exits.) They undoubtedly empty a park faster by at least an hour than if they created no urgency and let everybody meander out at their own chosen pace. Southwest Airlines figured out how to get their planes boarded much faster than other airlines by issuing colored boarding cards but not assigning seats, so each group is in a hurry—sometimes a stampede—to board, to get the best remaining seat. They create urgency. No, these are not marketing examples, but they are excellent demonstrations of the role that success or failure at creating urgency has in every kind of business.

Direct Marketing can often *contextually* provide opportunity to create urgency of immediate response. This can be done with limited supply, limit per household or buyer, the countdown clock you see on a direct-response TV commercial, or a webinar. If the product itself cannot be limited in supply, some bonus or premium attached to it certainly can be. In the seminar business, a place I live and work, we use the obvious devices like "early bird discounts" and extend-a-pay monthly installments tied to a deadline to motivate early registrations, but we also use bonuses, entries into prize drawings, backstage-pass opportunities, preferred seating, closed-door, limited-number luncheon tickets available only to the first 50 or first 100 to beat the deadline in order to create even more urgency. Retail mimics this with the "door buster sales" starting at 5 D.P., 6 D.P., or 7 D.P., and can plus that urgency with a gift for the first x-number to be there with noses pressed against the glass. Disney creates false limited supply by bringing a product like a movie DVD, in their language, "out of the Disney vault just until Halloween—then it goes back in the vault and can't be had." They periodically bring the same product out of the vault, run the same short promotion, return it to the vault, wait until consumers have forgotten about the promotion, then trot it out again. All these examples are about creating *a context for urgency of response.*

Direct Marketing can also *structurally* provide opportunity for urgency of response. Anytime a group dynamic can be applied, a stampede effect seen, an "act now or lose out forever" reality displayed, a higher percentage of people presented with an offer will act than will under any other circumstances. People are motivated to buy what they will not be able to get if they don't buy now, even when they would not buy now if relieved of that threat of loss. An auction is a prime example of this, and it has successfully been moved to online media with live and timed auctions on sites like eBay. Putting people "live" into a seminar room where a persuasive speaker makes an offer from the stage, citing limited supply or discount or gift only for the first x-number, and *having people see the stampede* of earliest responders rushing to the product table at the back of the room is hard to trump by any other means and impossible to perfectly replicate by any other means; however, we've learned to come close with live online webinars, where viewers can see the earliest buyers' comments, the "ticker" recording the purchase, the countdown clock for the closing of the shopping cart ticking away, and in live webinars, we can recognize by name the fast buyers. A direct-mail, fax, and/or email sequence that begins by announcing that only 47 of the whatever-product will be sold (at this price, in this color, with this bonus, etc.) can, in its 2nd piece, list the names of the first 18 buyers and show that only 29 remain, and in its 3rd piece list the names of the 34 buyers and show that only 13 remain available.

The most powerful urgency by exclusivity is having only one available. Neiman-Marcus does this every year, in the pages of its big Christmas catalog, with unique gift items and experiences that there is only one of. For example, in the 2012 Christmas book, they offered a backstage experience and actual walk-on part one night in the Broadway musical *Annie*, for just $30,000.00; a Woody Trailer re-configured as an elaborate portable bar, as the ultimate tailgate party vehicle, for $150,000.00; a private dinner for a party of ten with a gaggle of great celebrity chefs, for $250,000.00; and a trip for two to Paris and Geneva, including a visit to the Van Cleef & Arpels boutique and watchmaking shop, and unique his-and-her watches, for $1,090,000.00. Will someone buy each of these one-of-a-kind gifts? Based on historical precedent with NM's annual one-of-a-kind gifts, that answer is almost certainly: yes. But, really, anybody can create one-of-a-kind gifts and experiences, or very limited availability equivalents. NM also garners an enormous amount of media attention and free publicity each year because of these extraordinary gift offers—something a local business could do at a local level just as easily.

In B2B, in the advertising, consulting, and coaching fields, this is often done with geographic area exclusivity. A collection of licensed print ads and radio and TV commercials, a seat in a mastermind group, access to various resources becomes more desirable (and can be sold for a much higher price) when only one CPA in Pittsburgh can have it, thus the race is on and any delay may put it in the hands of your archcompetitor with you forever locked out than when it is available to any and all comers.

Certain businesses have actual scarcity. The people I acquire rare and first-edition books from for my collection, Bauman Books in New York, have actual scarcity and therefore real urgency. If they have a single copy of a first-edition book I want, signed by its author, I know they are simultaneously notifying multiple clients of its availability and even a minute's hesitation may let someone beat me to the purchase—so I must decide quickly and impulsively; I have no time to consider cost. Most businesses lacking such actual scarcity can, with creative thought, manufacture it, offer by offer by offer.

So, how could an ordinary local restaurant and sports bar create an exclusive offer with enormous inherent urgency, publicity appeal to local media, and excitment for its customers? My prescription would be to rent a football celebrity, perhaps a local hero, maybe not, and craft an afternoon and evening of activities around his presence. One offer, fairly standard: He's there for a meet 'n' greet and photo opportunity during the Sunday afternoon games for any customer with autographed footballs and jerseys auctioned off during an hour within that time frame, with proceeds to a local charity . . . a limited number permitted in, pre-registration made possible, with or without ticket fee. Then, the exclusive offer: Just 12 patrons can buy a ticket to go into the private dining room or roped-off section, have dinner with, watch the Sunday night game with, and hang out with the star, and get an autographed ball, jersey, and photo . . . at, say, $2,000.00 per ticket. With that, there's massive urgency because there are only 12. A financial advisor, lawyer, auto dealer, etc., etc., could utilize the same premise, renting the facility or joint-venturing with a restaurant owner, and still incorporating the local charity. The event itself would be directly profitable, reward good clients, create new clients. The "halo effect" of the promotion to the business's entire email, social media, and mailing lists is significant, the opportunity for free, but valuable publicity, profound. What's most important to understand is that I took a business that is about "come on in" and eat, drink, and be merry and converted it to a Direct Marketing business, with two different, specific offers, both with created and legitimate urgency.

My friend, top direct-response copywriter John Carlton, always advises imagining your prospective customer or client as a gigantic somnambulant sloth, spread out on the couch, loathe to move his sleeping bulk, phone just out of reach. Your offer must force and compel him to move now. Your goal is immediate response. A plain vanilla, dull, mundane offer won't do it.

CHAPTER 3

Obey Orders

hy don't we get the results we want from other people? Husbands and wives routinely complain about their spouses expecting them to be mind readers. Managers bemoan employees' failures to perform as expected, often saying, "But I told him once." Most managers' ideas about training omit a feedback loop to ascertain comprehension and acceptance, and ignore the need for perpetual reinforcement. Everywhere you look in human-to-human communication, there is disappointment. This certainly exists for marketers too, although many business owners don't think they should be able to outright *control* the behavior of their customers to the extent they should be able to employees, vendors, or family members. In marketing and sales, control is exactly what we need. Ultimately, all this is much about simple clarity. Do people really, clearly know what is expected of them? Or are you taking too much for granted, chalking things up as too obvious to bother clarifying?

Rule #3
You Will Give Clear Instructions

Most people do a reasonably good job of following directions. For the most part, they stop on red and go on green, stand in the lines they're told to stand in, fill out the forms they're given to fill out, applaud when the Applause sign comes on. Most people are well-conditioned from infancy, in every environment, to do as they are told.

Most marketers' failures and disappointments result from giving confusing directions or no directions at all. Confused or uncertain consumers do nothing. And people rarely buy anything of consequence without being asked.

When I held one of my mastermind meetings for one of my client groups at Disney, one of the Disney Imagineers we met was in charge of "fixing confusion." At any spot in any of the parks where there was a noticeable slowing of movement (yes, they monitor that) or an inordinate number of guests asking employees for directions, he was tasked with figuring out the reason for the confusion and changing or creating signs, giving buildings more descriptive names, even re-routing traffic as need be to fix the confusion. "It isn't just about efficient movement," he told us, "it's about a pleasing experience. People do not like not knowing where to go or even what is expected of them."

In-store signage, restaurant menus, icons on websites— everywhere you closely examine physical/selling environments and media—you will find plenty of assumptions about knowledge people have (and may not have) and plenty of opportunity for confusion. In a split-test in nonprofit fundraising by direct mail, four different business-reply envelopes were used: One was a standard pre-paid business reply envelope with the standard markings; the second was the same, but with a large hand-scrawl-appearing note, "No postage stamp needed. We've paid the postage. Just drop in the mail." Third, a plain, pre-addressed envelope with an actual stamp affixed. Fourth, the plain, pre-addressed envelope with an actual stamp affixed plus the hand-scrawl-appearing note, "No postage stamp needed. We've paid the postage. Just drop in the mail." To be fair, the last two add obligation to clarity, and they were the winners by a significant margin. But the first envelope was the biggest loser by a very big margin even against the second, simply because the first presumes knowledge on the consumer's part that is not there. Not long ago, I got a statistically meaningful increase in conversion of visitors to buyers at a website by switching from just a "Buy Now" button, to the button plus the words "Click This Button to Buy Now."

When you put together *any* marketing tool, ad, flier, sales letter, website, phone script, etc. or *any* physical selling environment, it should be carefully examined for presumption of knowledge on the consumer's part, for lack of clarity about what is expected of them, or for wimpiness about asking clearly and directly for the desired action. Stop sending out anything without clear instructions. As illustration, take a look at the copy on page 32, excerpted from an actual sales letter (sent to knowledgeable buyers already in a relationship with the marketer). Note that the subhead above the copy is *quite* clear.

It's also worth noting that people's anxiety goes up anytime they are asked to do something but are unsure of what to expect. In my book *No B.S. Guide to Marketing to Leading-Edge Boomers and Seniors*, in Chapter 15 ("The Power of Stress Reduction"), I share an example of a marketing device and copy we routinely use with professional practices, such as chiropractic, dental, or medical offices or financial advisors' or lawyers' businesses, titled, *"What to Expect at Your First Appointment."* Anxiety about anything uncertain grows more acute with age, but is not unique to boomers and seniors. Removing it with very clear instructions, directions, descriptions, or information is smart strategy.

Last, you should consider the physical device of the order form. The late, great direct-response copywriter Gary Halbert claimed to often spend as much time on the copy and layout of the order form as he did the entire sales letter. In one part of my business life, professional speaking and selling my resources in an in-speech commercial, I've taken great pains to create order forms that are passed out to the audiences, or at the rear-of-room product tables, that mimic the best mail-order order forms in completeness and clarity, and I credit my order forms with aiding me in consistently achieving exceptional results—including selling over $1 million of my resources from the stage per year, for more than ten years running. A lot of businesses don't even use order forms when they could and should. If you have a particular interest in this, you can see a collection of five model order forms, with comments, at www. NoBSBook.com/DirectMarketingBook.

In Direct Marketing, we have learned a lot about consumer satisfaction, which affects refunds in our world and at least repeat purchasing and positive or negative word-of-mouth in every business: Presented with "difficult" or complex products, many customers are quickly, profoundly unhappy. I cannot tell you the number of times I've received a product that disappointed by seeming more trouble than it's worth, and returned it or simply trashed it, and I am not alone. A friend of mine, often an early adopter, took her first iPad back to the store to ask for help, and was told by a disdainful clerk, "It's intuitive." Not to her. In direct-to-consumer delivery of complex products, we often add written labels to audio CDs or DVDs that *very clearly* state: Read/Listen/Watch This First. We sometimes even decal *the outside of* a box with, "Call This Free Recorded Message, Please, BEFORE You Open & Unpack Your <Insert Product Name>." We include a *simple* flow chart or "map" of how to use the product. Often, we have to "sell" the tolerance for complexity. One of my clients, Guthy-Renker, has the #1 acne treatment brand, Proactiv®, sold and delivered direct to the consumer. Although it's made clear in the advertising, a chief cause of consumer dissatisfaction and noncompliant use is that there are three bottles and a three-step process. *Three*. To many, two steps too many. If we don't persuade them that this is necessary and worth it, the product comes back for refund. You may not have actual refunds occurring, but more quiet dissatisfaction can be just as damaging.

Consumers like, are reassured by, and respond to clarity. Be <u>sure</u> you provide it.

The Power of Good Directions

Figure 3.1 on page 32 is actual "directions copy" from a sales letter, with the business identity removed. It has reinforced the scarcity/urgency established earlier in the letter. Given phone number, times to call, and persons they'll be speaking with, an alternative drive to a website is also included. In previous campaigns, this marketer had used a much simpler instruction—essentially "Call 000-000-0000 to place your order." The copy below more than tripled the response vs. the previously used instruction.

FIGURE 3.1: Sales Letter

What To Do Next

Only 14 of these xxxxxxxx's are available. This invitation was sent to 100 of our best customers—like you!—by Federal Express, to ensure everyone has received them at the same time and has fair opportunity to respond.
Without delay, please . . .

Call 000-000-0000 to secure one of these 14 xxxxxxx's. We will be accepting calls beginning at 7:00 A.M. on [Insert-Date] and continuing through Noon on [Insert Next Day's Date], or until all 14 are spoken for—whichever comes first. Helen or Rob will be available to personally take your call.

Or . . .

If you would like to see the xxxxxxxx, a 9-minute preview video is accessible online at www.[insert-site].com. You may also instantly purchase your xxxxxxxx online, at the conclusion of the video, and receive confirmation immediately.

As always, your satisfaction is guaranteed with a 15-day inspection and return privilege. All major credit cards accepted, and the convenience of three monthly installments on request.

CHAPTER 4

No Freeloaders

I was taught: Earn your keep. From a very young age, I had chores, I had work to do. When I discovered there was pricey coffee made from cat poop being sold—a demonstration included in my book *No. B.S. Price Strategy*—I sat the dog down for a discussion! Having everybody and everything earn their keep is deeply ingrained in me.

Anyway, most of us try to hold people accountable for assigned tasks, but a lot of businesspeople aren't as tough on the dollars they put to work in advertising and marketing. You've probably noticed, we are not living in the boom of 2006, 2007, or 2008, when money streamed uphill. If you were casual or deluded about waste or lack of accountability in advertising and marketing before, it's now the luxury you dare not afford.

Rule #4
There Will Be Tracking, Measurement, and Accountability

You are no longer going to permit *any* advertising, marketing, or selling investments to be made without direct and accurate tracking, measurement, and accountability.

You will be given all sorts of arguments against such a harsh position by media salespeople, by online media champions talking a "new" language of "new metrics" (see pages 81–88), by staff, by peers. You will smile and politely say, "Rubbish." Each dollar sent out to forage must come back with more and/or must meet predetermined objectives. There will be no freeloaders, there will be no slackers.

There are two reasons for this tough position.

First, because management by objectives is the only kind of management that actually works. When an NFL football team takes the field on Sunday, there are team objectives— not just winning, but for ingredients of victory that can be measured. Each player also has individual, measurable objectives that he and his coaches have discussed before the game and will evaluate after the game. So it should be when your team takes the field. Your team includes people you pay as well as marketing you pay for. You can't manage what you can't, don't, or won't measure. Vagueness must be banished.

I can tell you as ironclad fact that, of all my clients, past and present, the richest and most successful, the ones who build the best businesses, "know their numbers" better than all the also-rans. For a full discussion of the "money math" of business, I'll refer you to Chapter 43 of my book *No B.S. Guide to Ruthless Management of People and Profits.*

The second reason for direct measurement is that you need real, hard facts and data to make good, intelligent marketing decisions. Making such decisions on what you and your employees think is happening, feel, have a sense of, etc., is stupid. And you don't want to be stupid, do you?

So, let's talk about tracking response. This means collecting as much information as you can, useful in determining what advertising, marketing and promotion is working and what isn't, which offer is pulling and which isn't. Admittedly, this can be a bit tricky. For example, Ad #1 may pull in new customers at $122.80 in cost and Ad #2 at $210.00, so you might decide Ad #1 is the winner. But the average first six months' purchase activity of those coming from Ad #2 is $380.00; the average from Ad #1 only $198.00. Now, which is more productive? Further, 30% of those from Ad #2 may refer others, while only 10% of those from Ad #1 refer. Now, which ad is better?

Do not dare shrug this off as too complicated. Think. Set up systems to capture the data you need and set aside time for the analysis. If it's painful and confusing at first, the fog will clear, the difficulty will abate. You will make discoveries that enable you to make better decisions, better allocate resources, create better marketing messages, and grow your business without simply growing the marketing budget proportionately. In a mature business, this is how profits can be grown without growing revenue.

Warning: Employees can often be an obstacle to accurate tracking, sometimes out of laziness, sometimes stubbornness, sometimes for more Machiavellian motives, such as concealing their own ineffectiveness. If there's been little or no tracking until now, there will naturally be resistance to the added work and to the revealed facts.

As an interesting example of what can be revealed, consider a company I did some consulting for, with complex advertising and marketing bringing prospects to offices for one-to-one sales presentations. The salespeople were inflating their closing percentages, with cooperation of the receptionists, under-reporting the number of appointments occurring. When I instituted a gift with appointment into the marketing, the salespeople suddenly had to requisition the needed number of gifts for the appointments they took. Bill could no longer claim he was closing 6 out of 10 when really closing 6 out of 20 now that he needed 20 gifts. Of course, the salespeople quickly claimed that giving the gifts was bringing in poorer quality prospects, but a controlled test of another kind firmly disproved that. The really awful thing in all this for the business owner was a lot of prospects he'd paid to get were coming and going invisibly, thus no follow-up on prospects who failed to buy at first attempt was occurring. Installing an effective, multistep follow-up campaign comprised of direct mail, email, and, finally, phone, added over $1 million in revenue the first year.

One more example. A chain of stores with advertising that produced a lot of walk-ins had in place a process whereby the clerks were to ask everybody which ad in which media had brought them in, and stick-count it, day by day. Unfortunately, this was subject to an enormous amount of "slop." Employees didn't ask and randomly added to the count in different categories or put a lot of numbers in "Misc." A change was made, giving visitors a little survey card to fill out, pushed by huge in-store signage, entering them in a weekly drawing for good prizes—and suddenly, a lot of accurate data materialized, very contradictory to the data that had been collected or, often, just made up by the staff.

If you loop back and connect this to Rule #1, you'll find an important key to tracking: offers. Different offers can be made in different media, to different mailing lists, at different times. Offer and promotional codes can be assigned to coupons, reply cards, surveys, online order forms. Big direct-response advertisers on radio, like Lifelock and 1-800-Flowers, tie promotional codes to different talk radio hosts, that the consumer enters at the website to secure discounts or gifts, often as simply as entering the host's name: Rush or Glenn or Sean. The internet also offers the local merchant an opportunity to force better tracking. Pre-internet, a local restaurant advertising on several radio shows and in a couple newspapers, giving away a free appetizer with dinner, could only try to find out which ad brought a customer in by having the customer tell the waiter or waitress in order to get the free appetizer, and relying on the wait staff to accurately stick-count and report that collected information. Now the consumer can be driven to a different, clone website to download a coupon for the free appetizer, the coupons collected and tallied, and a much more accurate result obtained—plus the added benefit of capturing the names and email addresses of those visiting the site, maybe offering online reservation-making options to the consumer as well.

Tough-minded management of marketing (and of people) requires *knowing* things. Of course, hardly any tracking mechanism is perfect. The job is to get as close to perfect as you can so that you are getting the best information possible.

Rule #5
Only No-Cost Brand-Building

Great GKIC members of ours, Forrest Walden and Jim Cavale, the brilliant marketers behind the fast-growing national franchise organization of Iron Tribe Fitness Centers, www.irontribefitness.com, gave a presentation to one of my mastermind groups they participate in, of their new "branding campaign"—and as they introduced it as such, a collective groan was emitted by the other coaching group members. They all know better! And they were all confident that I would react badly to a brand-oriented ad campaign and marketing program. But not so in this case, because these smart guys incorporated Rule #4 throughout the entire campaign. Even on their billboards, there was not just a website to visit, but a promotional code to enter, tied only to the billboard, so its direct results could be tracked. Tracking by separate phone numbers, domain names, or promotional codes was built into every item, every media used, every step of this campaign. Also, they obeyed Rule #5, so they weren't actually buying the brand-building. They were letting direct response pay for it. They are exactly right in their approach, they are a stellar example everybody should look at (regardless of the industry you're in), and, because they get this, they are a force to be reckoned with in their industry where, frankly, really horrible advertising is the norm.

I am *not* opposed to brand-building, nor would I argue against the influence, power, and value of brand. My own business is connected to brands—my own name, me, myself, and I. Dan Kennedy is a brand well-known and well-respected in entrepreneurial and marketing environments. Go Google me and see all you can find. The "No B.S." brand attached to this very successful book series published by Entrepreneur Press also extends to five successful newsletters, a full catalog of resources (DanKennedy.com/Store), and stands as positioning for GKIC. Many of my clients have developed and own very valuable brands, like Proactiv® (the #1 acne treatment), HealthSource® (the #1 franchised network of more than 350 chiropractic clinics), Ben Glass Law (see Chapter 12), and even great single-location, local businesses like Diana's Gourmet Pizzeria (www.dianasgourmetpizzeria.ca), Gardner's Mattress And More (www.GardnersMattressAndMore.com), and Columbia Music Arts Academy (www.columbiaartsacademy.com).

By the way, you can create brand power for even the most mundane of commodities. Coca-Cola branded water—Dasani. Victoria's Secret branded undergarments. Omaha Steaks—steaks, Hale Groves Grapefruit—grapefruit. Dasani Water is an off-shelf product. Victoria's Secret, retail. Omaha Steaks and Hale Groves are direct marketers, via mail order and e-commerce. I am personally invested in Kennedy's Barber Club shops (www.kennedysbarberclub.com), Infusionsoft, a marketing automation software (www.infusionsoft.com), and Imperial Auto Castle, an upscale storage facility for luxury, exotic, and collectors' classic cars with concierge service (www.imperialautocastle.com)—all branding basic products and services.

I am *not* opposed to brand-building.

I *am* opposed to paying for brand-building.

Most small-business owners cannot afford to properly invest in brand-building. Most startups lack the patient capital and luxury of time required by brand-building. I do not believe it is a wise investment for small-business owners and entrepreneurs, nor do I believe it is necessary. Brand power can be acquired as a no-cost byproduct of profitable direct-response advertising and direct marketing. My preferred strategy is simple: Buy response, gratefully accept brand-building as a bonus. NEVER buy brand-building and hope for direct response as a bonus. (Unless you are actually trying to spend Daddy's fortune out of spite.)

Paying for traditional brand-building may be fine, even essential, for giant companies with giant budgets in combat for store shelf space and consumers' recognition. If you are the CEO of Heinz or Coors or some company like that, playing with shareholders' money, and fighting it out as a commodity purveyor, by all means buy brand identity. But if you are an entrepreneur playing with your own marbles, beware. Copying the brand-builders can bankrupt you. You should also take note of really big, brand-name companies that are advertising brand but also aggressively and directly asking prospects to go to a website or call a phone number, like GEICO and Progressive in insurance. Even companies with a lot of brick-and-mortar stores, who have built brand identity, like Sleep Number Bed, still do a lot of advertising offering free DVDs and literature sent to consumers calling an 800# or visiting a website. This direct-lead flow is paying for the advertising, with the contribution to brand recognition as a bonus. A relatively small percentage of brand-name advertisers know how to do this well, so you have to be very careful about who you model.

It's also worth noting that there's no guarantee of success or sustainability with widespread brand recognition and brand equity. Some once very famous and dominant brands are, today, badly tarnished, shadows of their former selves, or dead. In the motel industry, the leading American brands *were* Holiday Inn and Howard Johnson's. Pontiac was once a leading car brand in the GM portfolio, and for a time, Rambler was the brand that stood for reliability, and Rambler dominated the station wagon category. More recently, Borders was one of two top brands in bookselling. Some of the brands you know and perceive to be dominant leaders in their fields and product categories today will be diseased or dead within ten years. The graveyard of once powerful brands is big, and welcomes new arrivals frequently. Any idea of inevitability of an established brand is foolish and dangerous conceit.

Finally, there is a case for ignoring branding altogether, entirely or situationally. What I am about to reveal here is a very, very powerful advertising and marketing strategy very well-known to Direct Marketers but largely ignored or misunderstood by all others. It is the deliberate use of nakedly un-branded advertising.

What you never want to do is let brand-building get in the way of the most powerful and profitable advertising and marketing opportunities to grow your business. There are many types of direct-response lead-generation ads, designed to motivate qualified prospects for a particular product or service to step forward, identify themselves, and ask for information, that work much better "blind," absent any company name or logo or branding than they do with identity disclosed. One version is the now classic "Warning" ad:

Warning to Mutual Fund Investors
Expert Predicts Dramatic Change and
Danger in the Next 29 Days.
This Is Information You MUST Have—That
Brokers Don't Want You to Know. For Free
Information and "The Wall Street Secrets Report,"
call the Fund Investor Hotline at 1-800-000-0000 or
go online to www.SecretsHotline.com

You absolutely kill that ad's pulling power if you attach a big, fat logo, a national brand name, or a financial planning firm's name and slogan to it.

In this category, in financial and investment information publishing, one of the all-time biggest successes was a campaign that dominated print, radio, and cable TV in 2011 and 2012, driving traffic to an online video at EndOfAmerica. com. (You can probably still see it via YouTube). This ad was aired, seen, and heard so much the domain name itself nearly had brand identity, but throughout, neither the company nor its brand, the newsletter ultimately being sold, the author, or any other identity, corporate or personal, was disclosed in the advertising. It was completely "blind." I am told it broke all subscriber acquisition records of its company and probably the industry, bringing nearly a million new subscribers into the fold. Incidentally, as a side point, the online video was 90 minutes long, so let that stick a dagger in the persistent and erroneous beliefs about short viewer attention spans and/or need for short copy. But the point: Zero brand-building was attempted. If in the hands of most big, dumb companies in publishing, insurance, annuities, gold, or other financial goods and services, they and their nincompoop ad agencies would have insisted on mucking up the ads with their corporate names, logos, slogans, years in business.

You can always brand-build internally with customers once they are acquired. There's no law that says you can't create powerful brand identity and preference with customers yet never even mention it to new prospects.

There are even instances where a brand suppresses response *because of its virtues*. I have, on more than one occasion, had clients in niche markets who had become very well-known and well-respected, and if you asked 100 people in their market about them, nearly all of the randomly chosen 100 had generally positive things to say about the company but could also rattle off the five key components of that company's sales story and offerings. No mystique, no curiosity. A been-there-heard-that-done-that-before problem. Success came by trotting out "blind" advertising and marketing with fresh promises and bold positioning, which would have been instantly discredited if voiced by the venerable, old industry leader. Then, once interest in the promises was created, information could be provided that revealed the match of the biggest, most respected brand with the hot, new, daring products.

In short, brand is not necessarily the Holy Grail. Brand-building is best for very, very patient marketers with very, very deep pockets filled with other people's money. You are likely far better served by focusing on leads, customers, sales, and profits directly driven by your marketing, letting whatever brand equity you get be provided as a free byproduct of direct marketing.

Interview* with Rick Cesari: Brand-Building by Direct Marketing

Rick Cesari is the author of a must-read book on Direct Marketing, *BUY NOW: Creative Marketing That Gets Customers to Respond to You and to Your Product*, based on his extraordinary experience bringing products like The Juiceman, the Sonic Toothbrush, and The George Foreman Grill to market.

DAN KENNEDY: Monster successes like those you've shepherded never begin that way. They begin with proving we have something to sell and proving we can craft a message that people will respond to, starting by playing small ball. I'd like you to talk a little bit about the way you started these businesses, such as The Juiceman.

RICK CESARI: We started The Juiceman business in 1989, and in 3¹/₂ years we grew the sales from zero to $75 million. I found

Brand-Building by Direct Marketing, *cont.*

Jay Kordich, the inventor and personality of The Juiceman, at a small, local consumer show. 10' x 10' booths, people selling products. All the booths had one or two people, but this one booth had a crowd, 50 people gathered. Jay was there, talking about the health benefits of juicing, demonstrating his machine, and he had people captivated. I talked with him and found out he was living on the road, working these kinds of shows, state fairs, that sort of thing, all over the country, selling a lot of juice makers to groups. I'd already been in the direct marketing field a long time, and I was sure that we could take what he was doing on this small level, move it to media and build it into something a lot bigger.

DAN: I think it's important I point out: Jay had a small business, reaching small numbers of customers, by successful direct selling. With Direct Marketing, you could basically multiply him with media. The reason I push owners of businesses thought of as ordinary to move away from traditional marketing to Direct Marketing is that they can multiply what they do successfully one to one into one to many with media.

RICK: That's right. But we didn't run out and make TV infomercials immediately. We made calls to get Jay booked as a guest on local radio and TV shows, to talk about health and juicing. Our first breakthrough came on a New York station, on a local morning show hosted by Matt Lauer, who now, of course, is a *Today Show* host. Jay was on for 20 minutes and told people, if they would send in an envelope with a dollar, he'd send them recipes. I was told that the station switchboard lit up, but this was before the internet, so everything happened through the mail, and it took a week before we saw the result. He was on

Brand-Building by Direct Marketing, cont.

on June 30th. On July 6th, the mail truck pulls up, and the mailman brings in three canvas sacks. 12,000 envelopes with dollars in them. We sent out a flier selling juicers with those recipes and that's what started this business. We used that strategy, got Jay on show after show after show. We also started using those interviews, then our first infomercial to get people to come to free health seminars, where Jay would sell from the stage to hundreds and hundreds of people at a time.

DAN: Let's be sure everybody gets that there is architecture here that does not go out of date. This doesn't have an expire date on it.

RICK: This model still works, although we get to add the internet, we have more marketing tools—but Direct Marketing from more than 25 years ago with The Juiceman and the Direct Marketing we're applying to our latest projects is the same. There's a company, Go Pro Cameras, the little cameras that skiers and snowboarders wear on their helmets. They've grown from zero to $250 million in 3 years, and, basically, the same marketing model we used 25 years ago plus new media has been responsible for that success.

DAN: The next question goes to Message. Many businesspeople think that their products, services, or businesses are ordinary; they complain about commoditization and competition, and they just can't see how what you've done and do—how what they see with products sold direct in infomercials, in direct-mail packages—applies to them. When you think about, basically, a blender, a countertop grill, a toothbrush, it's hard to be more ordinary than these products, yet you take them to Direct

Brand-Building by Direct Marketing, cont.

Marketing, and turn them into multimillion dollar brands, and move them successfully to retail where they sell off the shelf. Let's talk a bit about this turning the ordinary into something very sellable and very exciting to the public—and let me emphasize the requirement of making whatever you offer, sell, do *exciting* to the public. You just can't afford to accept the idea that your thing is doomed to be ordinary and uninteresting, can you?

RICK: You have to look at products *in a different way.* In 1989, there *were* a lot of juicers being sold, but they belonged to appliance manufacturers and were being sold *conventionally* as kitchen appliances. The twist we put on it with Jay was to make it a health device, not a kitchen appliance. We never talked much about the blades or motor or size of container. We pushed the information booklets, the immune-trengthening diet, the weight-loss juice diet, anti-aging. When we brought the Sonic Care Toothbrush out, there was one other premium priced electric toothbrush sold through dentists, but there were quite a few sold to consumers for a few dollars. Sonic Care was $150.00. How to sell a $150 toothbrush? Nobody understood or cared about sonic technology. So we made our message about reversing gum disease, preventing heart disease, etc. With the George Foreman Grill, there were a lot of little grills, and it was actually originally a taco maker—it's slanted the way it is to slide the ground beef into the taco shell. Not surprisingly, it wasn't selling. We determined you could drain the fat and grease that way, and with George Foreman, made it about "Knock Out The Fat." Again, a health device, not just a kitchen appliance. There have been more than 30 million George Foreman Grills sold. We believe there is *always* a unique benefit.

Brand-Building by Direct Marketing, cont.

DAN: This is one of the differences between the way most businesspeople and marketers think versus the way we direct marketers think. They look to the product and its features for benefits to talk about. We want to be storytellers. We look for the hidden benefit, for the benefit that matches up with consumers' life issues and interests. Is the Go Pro camera the same sort of story?

RICK: Really, there's *nothing* special about the camera. Just the mounts. This company's growing dramatically and Kodak is dying, and Poloroid died. The Go Pro company founder figured out how to mount the camera with a wristband, chest strap, helmet mount, on a surfboard—so it's tied into all the extreme action sports. Social media is tied in, so users create YouTube videos and post on Facebook, and the company offers awards for the best videos. But if you take the camera, *anybody* can go make the camera.

*Excerpted from and based on an exclusive interview with Rick Cesari for the monthly GKIC Diamond Members' Tele-Seminar & Q&A Conference Call. For information about GKIC Membership featuring my *No B.S. Marketing Letter/Dan Kennedy Letter*, refer to page 175.

CHAPTER 5

No Holes in the Bucket

A business is a bucket in which alchemy is to occur. Into the bucket we pour ideas, energy, work, ad dollars, marketing dollars, costs of attracting customers, costs of pursuing sales in hope of stirring into profits, maybe wealth. Most business owners are very focused on the pouring into the bucket. Few focus on exactly what happens inside the bucket. That's supposed to take care of itself. But it doesn't. It's important to have a full and accurate understanding of the investments being made. It's then important to have a strategy in place for fully and comprehensively converting those investments to the greatest possible gains.

Rule #6
There Will Be Follow-Up

Often, I find business owners with more holes in their bucket than they've got bucket! People read your ad, get your letter, see your sign, find you online, etc., they call or visit your place of business, they ask your receptionist or staff questions, and that's it. There's no capture of the prospect's name, physical address, email address, and no offer to immediately send an information package, free report, coupons. This is *criminal* waste. I've been poor, so I abhor and detest and condemn waste. Just how much waste are you permitting to slop around in your business? Probably a lot.

You don't just pay for the customers you get when you invest in advertising and marketing. You pay a price for *every* call, *every* walk-in. *Every one.* Doing nothing with one is just like flushing money down the toilet. To be simplistic, if you invest $1,000.00 in an ad campaign and get 50 phone calls, you bought each call for $20.00. If you're going to waste one, take a nice, crisp $20.00 bill, go into the bathroom, tear the bill into pieces, let the pieces flutter into the toilet and flush, and stand there and watch it go away. If you're going to do nothing with 30 of those 50 calls, stand there and do it 30 times. *Feel it.* You probably won't like how it feels. Good. Remember that feeling every time you fail—and it is failure—to thoroughly follow up on a lead or customer.

How to Find an Extra Million Dollars
in Your Business

Could you use an extra million bucks?

If in doubt, ask your wife or kids about it. If put to a family vote, maybe to a vote of your vendors and bill collectors, I'll wager the answer is a yes. And, less facetiously, more practically, would your future benefit from getting an extra million dollars put into your 401(k) or SEP or other retirement savings account? Well, I'm happy to direct you to where that extra million is hidden inside your business. It's in the follow-up that isn't happening.

Many times, owners of profitable ad and marketing campaigns are terribly slothful about this. If they spend $1,000.00 to get 50 calls, only convert 5 to appointments, and only acquire 2 as customers—but worth $1,000.00 each, they turn $1,000.00 into $2,000.00 and are pretty happy about that. But each call cost $20.00. Forty-five didn't turn into appointments—that's $900.00. Nearly as much waste as profit. But the total reality is far worse than that. If, with diligent and thorough follow-up, another 5 appointments and 2 customers could be had, he's let $900.00 plus $2,000.00 slip through holes in his bucket. If each customer can be made to refer one and an endless chain of referrals created, the $2,900.00 in waste goes to $4,900.00, then $6,900.00, then $8,900.00, then $10,900.00. Let that happen once a month, it's $109,000.00 that should have been in the bucket that leaked out onto the floor. In 10 years, it's a million dollars. It's my experience that in just about any small business, over a ten-year term, there is at least one million dollars in lost money to be had. If you own a small business and would like to retire as a cash millionaire, here's your opportunity.

Here are some of the holes in business buckets, through which money leaks:

1. *As just described, the person who calls and asks question stays unknown, and gets no follow-up.* Remember, you paid for that person. If you don't capture his contact information so you can do follow-up marketing, you wasted your money.

2. *Little or no follow-up on leads obtained at trade or consumer shows.* This is particularly abysmal. In my most recent experiment at a big, local Home & Garden Show, I visited nine competing companies' booths, very clearly presented myself as a viable prospect for their products, made it clear I was not interested in lowest price, and made sure they had my complete contact information (except email, which I do not use).

   And what follow-up did I get? By mail? Zero. By phone? Zero. Each of those exhibitors paid to get me, then they did nothing with me.

3. *No follow-up on referrals.* When Betty says, "I told Billy about you. I hope he gives you a call," the correct response is *not*: "Thanks Betty. I hope he does, too." That's the common response, but it most certainly is not the correct response. You ask for and get Billy's address, so you can send him a copy of your book or information package, with a note mentioning Betty's recommendation or a note from Betty, and an offer or offers (Rule #1). If Billy fails to respond, you send him a second letter. And a third, fourth, fifth. With offers. And you put him on your newsletter list and send him your monthly newsletter. With offers. You enroll him in your six-week email "course" tied to your product or service. That's follow-up.

4. *No instant follow-up to new customers.* Newly acquired customers need to become frequent and habitual repeat purchasers or ascend to higher levels of membership or somehow move from first transaction to committed relationship. This means they need to be quickly thanked, welcomed, and brought back, moved up, or otherwise committed. Think about the

last five times you patronized a business for the first time—store, restaurant, service company, professional practice. What formal thank-you did you get? In four or five out of five, none. What "welcome to the family" gift did you get?

5. *No prevention or rescue related to lost customers.* For more than 30 years, surveys have consistently revealed "indifference by provider" as, by far, the #1 reason customers leave a business and drift elsewhere. Not some egregious act of incompetence or negligence or insult, not cheaper prices, not anything major. Just a sense of

FIGURE 5.1: Holes in the Bucket

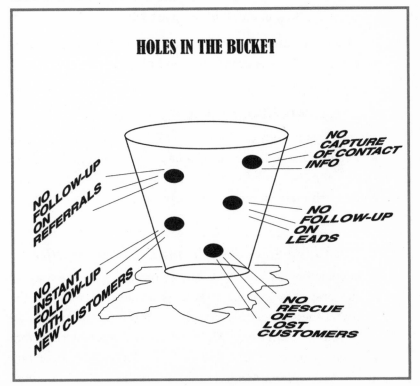

indifference toward them. That left them open to easy seduction. The best answer to lost customers is, of course, not having any. That requires very frequent, very consistent, and interesting online and offline communication. I teach 52 contacts a year, although I do more and GKIC does more. But on-time rescue efforts also work. Every kind of business has a set time by which a customer should be back: for the clothing store, it's once before each season; for the diner, it might be every morning; for the auto salesman, every three years.

Whatever it is for you, alarm bells should go off for every customer not back before his stamped-on expiration date, and that alarm should set in motion a flurry of marketing and follow-up activity.

There are other holes. I've just named five. You have to find every hole in your business and plug it.

What Does Follow-Up Look Like?

There are hundreds of variations of follow-up campaigns and strategies. One of the most reliable is structured in four main steps—although, mixing in low- and no-cost online media like email, each main step may have a handful of contacts, not just one.

Step 1: Re-State, Re-Sell, and Extend Same Offer

Whatever they didn't do or buy is presented to them again in the best way possible. There is acknowledgment at the start that they are getting your letter or other communication because they didn't buy. The message will acknowledge that there are x-number of reasons people don't respond or buy at the first appointment, visit, conversation, etc., and these reasons are then answered and made to go away. The original offer is made available, with a new deadline for response.

Step 2: Stern or Humorous "2nd Notice" Tied to Onrushing Deadline

Classic themes and opening gambits include the good-humored, "Are You Lost?" or, "Frankly, I'm Puzzled" to the serious and stern, like "I'm Deeply Concerned About Your Failure To . . ." or "Are You a Man or a Mouse?" The offer is again presented, the deadline emphasized. Sometimes, the offer is slightly altered, perhaps with longer installment financing or a new or additional gift with purchase.

Step 3: "Third and Final Notice"

This ties to the deadline and the disappearance of the offer. For a pest control company offering termite control to its route customers, I designed this Final Notice to come from the company's attorney, in a law firm envelope, explaining that, in order to safeguard the pest control company from any liability for negligence in not fully protecting its customers' homes, it was required to clearly notify them of the hazards and costs of failing to treat a home with termite protection.

One great example of a good-natured sequence covering these three steps is in my book *The Ultimate Sales Letter (4th Edition)*—the famous Giorgio Italian Restaurant letter sequence.

This has been a Direct Marketing staple for a long, long time. The very first Direct Marketer of the very first (albeit dubious) "cure" for what we now gently call E.D., or erectile dysfunction, Dr. J. R. Brinkley, a turn-of-the-century promoter of goat testicles grafts to men, generated leads by radio, print advertising, direct mail, and publicity, asked them to travel from hither and thon to his clinic, and followed up on the recalcitrant prospects with sequences exactly as described here. His marketing was so fascinating and so far ahead of its time and so remarkably effective, Chip Kessler and I wrote an entire book about it, rich with actual samples of Brinkley marketing gleaned from a historical society's archives: *Making Them Believe: The 21 Lost Marketing Secrets of Dr. J. R. Brinkley.*

Step 4: Change the Offer

Sometimes the offer can be altered relatively easily by offering new or more extended installment payment terms, by swapping out a bonus for a different bonus, that sort of thing. Other times, the unconverted prospects are telling you they don't like your solution to their need, interest, or desire. That doesn't mean the need, interest, or desire is gone. Mary responded to your ad because she wanted to lose two dress sizes before her friends' annual July 4th beach party. You offered her six weeks of supervised exercise in a gym. She rejected you. She still wants to lose two dress sizes by July 4th. She doesn't want to come to a gym three times a week. She might buy at-home personal training or a diet plan or pills or a gadget. Some business owners are limited to Steps #1–#3 and, as a practical matter, can't do #4. But a lot more can, if they would, than do. Trade schools began offering the option of online training for this reason. The "online university industry" pioneered by Phoenix University is a response to the same rejection of offer but continued desire for solution with regard to post-high-school education, career training, and degrees. Weight Watchers, famous for weekly meetings complete with weigh-ins, also added the alternative of online coaching and support for the same reason. Big direct marketers in the same interest category achieve this 4th step by swapping lead lists. People who respond, for example, to advertising about a money-making opportunity in real estate and stubbornly reject the offer are turned over to a marketer of a money-making opportunity in homebased e-commerce in exchange for that marketer's list of prospects who have rejected his offer.

Important Reminder: Obey ALL the Rules

All your follow-up efforts by any and all means—even direct conversation by phone or face to face—should adhere to all ten of the Rules that I'm presenting.

CHAPTER 6

Shouting Louder

aul Revere purportedly rode through the streets ringing a bell and yelling "The British are coming!" and everybody lit their candles or lamps and paid attention. He'd have little effect today. That was then, this is now. We are immune to noise. It's ever harder to get and hold attention just by making a lot of noise. If that worked, the marketers with the biggest bull-horns would always win and would stay on top forever, yet with increasing frequency little upstarts unseat longevity brands and category giants. There is also the matter of message, once attention is attracted. Certainly if you bang on my door loudly enough, persistently enough, I'll come to the door—but now, you'd damn well better have something fascinating and compelling to say.

Rule #7
There Will Be Strong Copy

Confronted with clutter, confusion, competition, and commoditization in the marketplace, many business owners respond by trying to shout louder. They may do this by spending more money, buying bigger ad space, advertising in certain media more frequently, hiring celebrity spokespersons or curbside clowns to wave placards. *But yelling isn't selling.*

I began business life as a salesman. Many business owners do not have such beginnings, and they are often handicapped by lack of experience with and poor attitudes about strong salesmanship. I morphed into a very successful career as a direct-response copywriter, and for the past decade or so, I've been paid no less than $1 million a year to craft and write copy that sells. I know that sales and subtlety rarely go hand in hand. I often find myself helping clients get over emotional hang-ups about this, the most common having to do with either an erroneous, often ego-driven belief that their clientele is more sophisticated than most and will not respond to "pushy" and sensational copy, or a fear of what people will think of them—those people not customers but peers, employees, friends, family, or the public at large.

The fact is, there is enormous, ever-growing, almost overwhelming competition for attention and interest, a daily tsunami of clutter that must be cut through or circumvented, even a dull-wittedness and numbness toward advertising, marketing, and sales messages that block reception in the same way driving into a dark underground tunnel blocks cell-phone reception. In this environment, the ordinary and normal are ignored, the cautious and calm messages, unnoticed.

You can't send a shy, timid Casper Milktoast to knock on the door of a home or walk into a business and beg in nearly a whisper for a few minutes of the prospect's time. So you can't do that with a postcard, letter, flier, newsletter, email, web video, etc., either. Send The Incredible Hulk instead—huge, glowing neon green, stomping, yelling. He can't be ignored. He shows up, guy drops what he's doing and pays attention. But there's a caveat . . .

Copy: The words in printed or online media can't *just* shout. Loud but irrelevant isn't much better than quiet and relevant. Loud, you can grab attention, but you can't convert it to interest. The Incredible Hulk stomping into your office would get your attention, but he'd still have trouble bridging to interest and having you engage in a conversation with him about a new copier. We have to be sensational and attention-commanding, but we have to do it in a way that establishes relevance and credible authority, and creates proactive interest in our information, goods, and services.

The Four Chief Sales Copy Mistakes (That Smart DIRECT Marketers Do Not Make)

Most great sales copy is written backwards, from the customer's interests, desires, frustrations, fears, thoughts, feelings, and experiences, journeying to a revealing of a solution or fulfillment tied to your business. Most ineffective copy starts, instead, with the company, product or service, and its features, benefits, comparative superiority, and price. These are the five default positions that the overwhelming majority of advertisers, copywriters, and salespeople fall back to, rather than developing a more creative, customer-focused positioning.

As example, consider these two appeals to golfers:

Now—You'll Hit The Ball Off The Tee
Farther And Straighter
Than You Ever Have In Your Life—
Each And Every Time
With "Perfect Swing"

Or:

Now—You'll Amaze Your Golf Buddies
When You Hit The Ball
Off The Tee
Farther and Straighter
Than You Ever Have In Your Life—
Each And Every Time
With "Perfect Swing"

Look closely. I only added four words expressing one key customer-focused benefit.

The first headline is about two benefits. The second is about an ego-rewarding experience you'll have because of the benefits. We could make it even more overt and stronger:

Now—You'll Be
The Envy Of
Your Amazed Golf Buddies
When You Hit The Ball
Off The Tee
Farther and Straighter
Than You Ever Have In Your Life—
Each And Every Time
With "Perfect Swing"

The first mistake is to rely on any or all of the five default positions instead of writing to and for and about the psyche of the customer.

As an aside, a quick "bonus" graphics lesson: Line breaks in ad copy matter. I've carefully picked the end words and start words of each line in the above headlines, so each line is a complete idea. If I leave it up to my computer to break the lines, they end in mid-thought.

The second, closely related mistake is writing factually and "professionally" rather than emotionally, with enthusiasm, and conversationally, as you would tell somebody about your discovery. I don't care if you are selling to Fortune 1000 CEOs in sky-high boardrooms or to Papa Bear in his mobile home in the trailer park, your best approach is to write like you talk, and like you and he would talk—and to infuse your writing with enthusiasm and with deeply emotional appeals.

In the above examples, the first version had no emotional appeal. The second, the emotional appeal of greater confidence, capability, and fun; a better experience to be imagined, and the mental picture produced is of you swinging the club perfectly and watching the ball soar long and straight and true. But in the third example, that emotional appeal is secondary to the much stronger emotional appeal of doing that while observed by amazed and envious friends.

The third mistake is being timid or bland in your claims and promises. I did not, in the above examples, stop at far and straight or farther and straighter. I made it: farther and straighter *than you ever have in your life*. Many believe that their customers, clients, or patients are smarter and more sophisticated than others, at least immune to such sensationalism and hyperbole, possibly offended by it, and that they might be discredited if engaging in it. Such business owners are wrong. Their beliefs are in contradiction with facts. In every category of product or service, in media directed at presumably educated and sophisticated people, I can find for you a highly sensational ad making grandiose and extraordinary claims that is a huge success. Zig Ziglar was right: "Timid salesmen have skinny kids"—no matter who they're selling to.

The fourth mistake is violating Rules #1 and #2. Too much copy wimps out at the point of directing the reader, listener, or viewer in exactly what they are supposed to do.

If you insist on shouting a weak message louder, you only ruin your vocal cords and dissipate energy. More aggressively advertising a weak message wastes money. You can even do lasting damage by marking yourselves in minds as timid and ordinary and uninteresting.

Now I have some news for you that you may well consider "bad news." Many people sabotage themselves a lot by categorizing facts as either bad news or good news, rather than just as facts to be appropriately acted on. A negative attitude toward a fact makes it worse news. The fact about strong sales copy is that you need it, and you may need to learn to write it for yourself. The very small fraternity of top-level direct-response copywriters like me are in high demand and are routinely paid upwards from $15,000.00 to $25,000.00 to write copy for one ad, letter, or website, upwards from $100,000.00 to write copy for a complete multimedia project, often with royalties linked to results on top of fees. We are a bargain for clients with sufficient size and scope of opportunity but unaffordable to most. There is, frankly, a precipitous drop from us to a large legion of journeyman freelance writers who present themselves as copywriters but often have little or no Direct Marketing experience or acumen.

Most small-business people who have strong copy in their marketing learn to write that copy for themselves. If this happens to be brand-new to you, start with my book, The *Ultimate Sales Letter (4th Edition)*, my *Magnetic Marketing System*® (DanKennedy.com/Store), and a few books on copywriting by the following people: Joe Sugarman, Michael Masterson, and classics by Robert Collier and Victor Schwab. The good news is, you will quickly see, by comparing the examples I gave you in this chapter and the examples in these recommended books and resources, where and how your copy is weak and how you can strengthen it—in many cases with minor yet significant changes, just as I did here with the golf example.

If, however, you prefer seeking help from outside, professional copywriters, you should check out the directories and jobs boards where you can post assignments and needs provided by American Writers & Artists, at awaionline.com. If you are in information marketing, publishing, seminars and conferences, or coaching and consulting, there are AWAI-Member freelance writers who have completed a Certification Program with me, specifically preparing them to serve such clients. You can access their directories via info-marketing.org or awaionline.com. Of course, if you think you might be an appropriate client for me, you're welcome to query my office via fax: (602) 269-3113.

CHAPTER 7

Tux, Tails, and Top Hat or Coveralls and Work Boots?

Businesspeople like fancy advertising. They like to dress up their advertising in marketing, in professional or elegant attire, and they are easily persuaded to do so by purveyors of fancy. Business owners love hearing praise for the cleverness, cuteness, or comedy of their marketing. Their egos are not concerned with results, but with feeling good and proud. As direct marketers, we prefer work clothes. We're not dressing up our marketing for approval by snobs at the fancy dress ball. We're getting it dressed and ready to do a job.

Rule #8
It Will Look Like Mail-Order Advertising

In the last chapter, copy. Next, appearance. Fortunately for you, Direct Marketing revolves around only a short list of Rules that I'm presenting here, and Direct-Response Advertising revolves around an even shorter choice list of formats. It is to look a certain way.

This is going to shock many of you to your core. It can, if you let it, simplify your life and make you a great deal of money. This Rule is a great simplifier, because it ends your paying attention to—and trying to emulate—the overwhelming majority of all the advertising you see on TV, in magazines, in newspapers, online; by your peers and competitors. You are to go blind to anything except pure mail-order advertising, which I'll tell you how to identify, and where to find, to observe, in a minute. But first, this is very important: All advertising except mail-order advertising will, from here on out, be willfully ignored. You will resist any temptation whatsoever to borrow from any of it, copycat any of it, worry about differences between it and your approach. You will, in fact, live in utter defiance of its norms.

I am specifically speaking of the formats, layout, and appearance of advertising—whether a print ad or a website or any other item. Classic pictorial mail-order ads are typically broken up into one-quarter, one-half, and one-quarter of the page, give or take. The top one-quarter is for headline and subheads; the middle half for presentation of product or proposition, sometimes aided by testimonials; the bottom one-quarter for the offer and clear response instructions, often with a coupon. The most frequently used alternative is the advertorial, which mimics an article. If you will stick with these two formats, you can safely ignore all others. Online, the homepage of a website mimics the classic ad: There are headlines and subheads at top, some product or proposition info in the middle, and a click to order, a form to fill in, an email box to fill in, at bottom. This may be assisted with video. It may *not* be polluted with top, side or bottom panels offering a myriad of click options taking visitors hither and thon and putting them in control of an experience full of variables. It will be the start of a single, focused sales presentation leading to a decision, response, or purchase instructions, and an action—just like a print ad.

To see real mail-order advertising, you need to assemble a diverse assortment of magazines in which many highly successful mail-order companies consistently run full-page advertisements. These include *Reader's Digest Large Print Edition*, Farm Bureau journals, tabloids like *National Enquirer* and *Star*, business publications like *Investors Business Daily, Entrepreneur, Small Business Opportunities*. As of this writing, mail-order companies running full-page classic, pictorial ads include the Jitterbug Phone, Sleep Number Bed, and the now iconic Amish-Made Heaters. There are many, many others. You will also encounter advertorials in the same publications. Tear out and keep these ads, *discard all others*. Let these true mail-order ads be your only models.

I also want you to seek out—Google, Amazon, etc.— the following legendary mail-order men: Joe Sugarman, Gerardo Joffee, E. Joseph Cossman. Get their books. Study their ads. These men know how to format a mail-order ad. For contemporary examples in diverse fields, visit all the websites I've listed for you in Section III, Resources. These are clients and students of mine and GKIC members* in diverse types and categories of business who have made their online and offline marketing look like and function like mail-order advertising. (*To join them, sign up for the offer on page 175.)

As you come to recognize the main mail-order ad formats (and everything else that isn't), you should build what direct marketing pros call "swipe files" for yourself, filled with sample ads torn from different magazines and newspapers, downloaded from the web, retained from mailings—only the mail-order-style ads. When you go to create something for yourself, you can review these samples for inspiration, ideas, and to keep you inside the box of mail-order ad appearance.

Understand, what I am telling you to do is "strange." On its surface, it is akin to telling you to put your automobile in storage and drive a boat to and from work on city streets. Others who see you using mail-order ad formats for your business will think you as batty as if you were driving a boat down the highway. That's okay. There's method to the madness . . .

First, only mail-order ads actually persuade people to buy things and to do so immediately and directly. Presuming you would like to sell things with your ads, I suggest it's not *really* strange at all to emulate only the ads that sell, rather than emulating all kinds of ads that do not sell. Other ad formats and styles may brand-build, please the eye aesthetically, be praised as creative, win critical acclaim and awards, affect market share over time, immeasurably and uncertainly influence, plant thoughts that later influence purchasing. But only mail-order ads sell.

Second, sticking with mail-order ad formats prohibits a lot of mistakes. I was at a writers' conference recently and listened to a much-published novelist, kicking out new books in three different series every six months, as she explained that she put her characters only in places she knew well, confined herself to plots she used repetitively, and basically operated within a small box. Someone asked her what would happen if she let herself out of her box? She said: many, many, many bad things. The same is true for the business owner or entrepreneur who is somewhat the amateur at direct marketing and direct-response advertising. If you let yourself roam outside a small box, you are vulnerable to being led astray in a dozen different directions, to winding up with "cool" and creative websites and ads that don't sell. You have two boxes: the classic, pictorial mail-order ad and the advertorial. Stay inside those two boxes.

As encouragement, let me show you a very simple and straightforward example of mail-order style-advertising for an ordinary, local business: landscaping. If you made a point of finding all the Yellow Pages, newspaper, magazine, direct-mail, Valpak and online advertising from the landscapers in your area, it's unlikely any would look like the one on page 73. Instead, they'd be full of photos and illustrations, and the company names, logos, and lists of services, and would look like a professionally prepared ad, like all other ads—a guy in black tuxedo amid a lot of other guys in black tuxedos at a wedding reception or charity ball. A bunch of penguins. This ad is the lone guy who wandered in, in plaid flannel shirt, denim coveralls, and work boots. Can't miss him.

Now here's the story behind this ad (see Figure 7.1 on page 72, reprinted from my MILLION DOLLAR MARKETING LESSON that appears monthly in *The No B.S. Marketing Letter*, this from September 2012).

FIGURE 7.1

Dan Kennedy's

MILLION DOLLAR MARKETING LESSON
Class is in session. The Professor of Harsh Reality and Grand Opportunity is here.

My Platinum Member Mike McGroaty wears denim coveralls, says "aw shucks", and plays at being "just a dumb dirt farmer." He is anything but. He has built and runs a successful farm, nursery and landscaping business, and has a thriving info-business, teaching "backyard nursery operation" to hobbyists and home-based businesspeople, for fun 'n profit. Here is an inspirational lesson in direct marketing that every local bricks-n-mortar or service business owner can profit from....

The Million Dollar Lesson, in Mike's own words:

"Dan, I recently ran this ad to see if it still worked – I haven't used it *since 1996* **(EXHIBIT #2)**. I guess I wanted to prove to the local Chapter/Mastermind Members that simple, straight-talk ads like this still work – I see them struggling with cluttered ads that won't produce and a lot of time-sucking online activity they can't measure. I ran this – again, RECENTLY – in a local, community newspaper, with about 50,000 circulation, for $400.00. It's written to repel more than it attracts. Those who can't spend $2,000 don't call. Those who live in $300,000 or $400,000 'mansions' don't call. Its target is the retired blue collar folks, in modest homes, in the working class neighborhoods, age 57 and up. 14 people called and we did 2 jobs. (We video taped one and I'm now going to make a how-to product out of this. Most of these re-landscape jobs can be done in under 6 hours with 3 guys, and the operator can net about $900.00 As you say, no reason to be broke in America.)

The history of this ad goes back to 1983, when I was tired of working for really arrogant people with money AND I was broke. I wanted quick, easy jobs that I could do in one day, not over three weeks. I started with a small ad (shown on page 69 of my book*) and it worked. I ran it in a coupon book 6 times a year *for 13 years,* with a 20-1 ROI. I went to the library to learn WHY it worked and found the book 'Tested

Advertising Methods', and I've been a student of marketing ever since. This ad is an expansion of the original, and as I just proved, it, and the old-fashioned newspaper, still work just fine.

[*Mike's book, *Can Any Small Business Make You Rich?* Is available at TurnTheCrankMarketing.com. You should read it. If you have a "young entrepreneur and future millionaire" in the family, it's great for him or her too.)

By the way, the Mailbox Million Training, great stuff. My biggest takeaways haven't sunk in yet, but the one thing that resonated with me was: 'you can sell people things they AREN'T searching for.' In my info-marketing business, hardly anybody goes online searching for what we sell, but when you said it at Mailbox Millions, it really hit home. Also, that I need to focus on the 5% who will pay more and the 1% who will pay a lot more. With 100 new customers a week, we are leaving a lot of money on the table."

Now, a caveat. This ad operates in contradiction to Ben Glass' advice elsewhere in this issue of The No B.S. Marketing Letter, where he says "the purpose of your ad should not be to make a sale. That's making the ad do too much work." Ben advocates lead generation and follow-up by media (not manual labor), to lead to the sale – also the approach I usually prefer and champion. Ah, but, there is more than one way to be right. And marketing choices are situational, not universal or absolute. Technically, even Mike's ad is lead generation, with a free offer (for estimate and design), but Mike also has his ad doing a lot of heavy lifting, nearly making the sale, disclosing price. This is why we test different approaches, and show you different approaches, so you can get to a customized 'ultimate marketing plan' that perfectly suits you. Ben is one of the smartest professional practice marketers there is on Planet Dan or anywhere else, but he and I and everyone else must be used as guides, not dictators.

■■■■■

Article reprinted from the MILLION DOLLAR MARKETING LESSON, *The No B.S. Marketing Letter*, September 2012.

FIGURE 7.2

Your House Re-Landscaped
Only $1,995!

Just look at everything you get for this crazy low price!

First of all, the consultation, the estimate and the design are free. You won't pay a dime unless you hire me to actually do the work. I will design a landscape that not only compliments the architecture of your home, but a landscape that is pleasing, colorful, interesting, and very, very easy to care for. This design will include an array of beautiful plants, all hand selected at the nursery by me. I'll show you photos of the plants that I am proposing for your home and I will give you a written, signed estimate.

If you hire me to do the work this is what you can expect to happen:

We'll come out and rip out all of the old shrubbery in front of your house and haul it away. I will personally layout the planting beds with a gentle design of sweeping curves that will be attractive and very easy to navigate with a lawn mower.

All weeds and grasses will be removed. We'll then wheelbarrow by hand, (no machines tearing up your lawn!) a minimum of five cubic yards of good, rich topsoil into the planting beds.

Once the planting beds are prepared the new plants will be brought in and very carefully arranged before they are installed, making sure each plant is precisely placed in the landscape. Once planted I personally do any pruning that is necessary so the finished landscape looks great and you won't have to touch it all summer!

We'll finish up by applying two to three inches of hardwood bark mulch and then I've got a secret weed control strategy that works incredibly well to keep your new landscape free for many months to come.

That's it! You don't have to lift a finger. The most work you'll do is picking up the phone to call.

When we are completely finished we'll clean up and make sure there is nothing left for you to do. As I mentioned earlier we haul away all of the debris.

That's what you get for $1,995.

Wait! That's not all.

You also get a no questions asked one-year guarantee on every single plant.

FIGURE 7.2 continued

Your House Re-Landscaped Only $1,995!

That' right, if you lose any plants in the first twelve months I'll come out and replace them free of charge! Seriously. All of the plants are guaranteed to live for one full year.

There are a couple of other things you should know. One, I'll be on the job working right along with my crew. I am not going to send a bunch of unsupervised knuckleheads to your house. I just won't do that!

I'll be there with my son Duston. Duston has been working with me for years and he knows as much about this as I do. We'll probably bring somebody else along as well to help with some of the heavy work.

As much as I love doing these re-landscape jobs, they are a lot of work and as much as I hate to admit it, swinging a spade, a spud bar, and pushing a wheelbarrow all day kicks my baby boomer butt! I need a lot more breaks that I used to, that's for sure!

But I truly enjoy doing these re-landscape jobs. I love the people I work for, and I love the look on their faces when the jobs are done.

The other thing that you should know is that we don't mess around. We are not going to come to your house, make a mess then disappear for days or weeks at a time. Once we start we stick with it until it's done unless the weather forces us to postpone for a day. But won't leave you in a mess. We'll get in, get it done, and get out!

You will be very, very pleased when we are done. I promise!

Okay, now here's the catch. I've only got time to do a few of these re-landscapes. I might do three of them, maybe four, absolutely no more than five. If you're interested I suggest you call right now.

Remember, there's no obligation, the estimate and design are free.

Michael J. McGroarty
McGroarty Enterprises Inc.
Perry, Ohio 44081
440-223-5309

P.S. I really am only going to do a few of these. Wish I could do more, but you know . . . Time is the elusive monster.

Reprinted from the MILLION DOLLAR MARKETING LESSON, *The No B.S. Marketing Letter*, September 2012.

CHAPTER 8

Money in the Bank

In any and every business, you're actually in
a number of businesses. Most businesses have many
deliverables, not one. A dental practice may be in the teen-
age teeth-straightening business with products from traditional
braces to Invisalign®, but also in the implant business with
seniors. Each business is the same. A quantum leap in income
occurs when an entrepreneur differentiates deliverables from
business, and sees himself in the marketing business. An even
more profound shift in thinking takes us to being in the money
business. It is possible to be in business for reasons other than
money, but it's rarely a good idea, and it's usually more accurate

to term such endeavors hobbies and tax losses. Most business owners are, above all else, acknowledged or not, in the money business. There is a relationship between your acceptance of that fact and behaving accordingly and the amount of money you make. When you fully grasp that you are in the money business, you think, behave, and govern differently than when you think you are in some other business—and your income automatically improves.

Rule #9
Results Rule. Period.

Consider the simple agreement: You want your car hand-washed and waxed outside, vacuumed out inside, for which you will pay your neighbor's teen $20.00. If he does not wash or wax or vacuum the car but wants the $20.00 anyway, what possible "story" could he offer in place of the result of a clean car that would satisfy you? I would hope none. You didn't offer to pay for a story. You offered to pay for a clean car. The same is true with advertising and marketing investments, and do not let anyone confuse, bamboozle, and convince you otherwise.

Further, no *opinions* count—not even yours. Only results matter.

One of the best things about Direct-Response Advertising and Direct Marketing is that we can run split tests and tests against controls. If I have two ideas for positioning and promoting the same product or place of business—let's say one has to do with the organic and health benefits of the food, the other with the gourmet and exotic nature of it, the "cool" factor—I can create two ads or just two different headlines for the same ad, and test them in the same environment. On the internet, I must use Google AdWords. I might drive traffic from the same source to two different websites. Offline, I might split a mailing list in half. I might put a freestanding insert about idea #1 in half a day's newspapers, and FSI (free standing insert) about idea #2 in the other half. By adhering to Rule #4, I will then *know* which produces more and better response. I don't have to settle for anything less than *knowing*. That's a split-test. If you have an ad, a Val-Pak coupon, a postcard, a website, anything that works satisfactorily, in direct-marketing industry lingo, you have a control piece. We test one variable at a time against that control, in split tests. Again and again and again, as often and as cheaply as we can. When a change boosts response, it is incorporated into a new control.

Either way, we arrive at a definite factual conclusion provided by actual results. This negates any and all opinions.

If you operate a very small business and can't figure out how to do much of this kind of testing, then the next best thing is to pay very, very close attention to national direct marketers selling comparable ideas, goods, or services to your customers, because they are doing a lot of testing, and their controls are visible. If, for example, you are a doctor or a hospital, you would pay very close attention to the health and alternative health newsletter publishers and the nutritional supplement companies who market by direct mail, radio, TV, and online— and it is easy to get on all these mailing lists and get all their mail; just subscribe and buy from a few. Use different versions of your name (Dan Kennedy; Dan S. Kennedy; Daniel Kennedy; etc.) and different addresses (your office; your home; your parents) so you get multiple copies of the same mailings and can more easily determine whether a particular piece is being mailed expansively, often and repetitively over months, marking it as a control. People like my friend Brian Kurtz at Boardroom sell millions of dollars of health-related "cure" books and newsletters by direct mail, spend tens of millions of dollars mailing their sales materials, and run umpteen split tests and tests against controls. Their test results can be yours to use. The same thing exists in almost every product, service, need, interest, or subject matter category. There are direct marketing leaders selling to your customers. You can also access on-demand archives of current and historical controls in any category via InsideDirect-Mail.com.

Back to health: If five different smart direct marketers' controls all feature, as a bonus with purchase, a book, report, or CD about remedies for joint pain—even though some are selling books, others newsletters, others pills, and none are selling a joint pain remedy, and they are mailing to consumers age 50 to 70, and you have any kind of a local health practice and want to attract patients age 50 to 70, and you fail to create an offer as a gift a book, report, or CD about remedies for joint pain, you are a blockhead.

If you can combine leveraging other marketers' test results by studying and extracting common success factors from their controls with your own testing, you can develop "killer" promotions, campaigns, marketing materials, websites, and web videos. Yes, I'm afraid this requires you to become a serious student, observer, and analyst of top direct marketers successfully selling to your customers and prospects. Yes, it requires you to actually work to elevate your game. No, there's no one magic app for this. But if you sincerely want to raise yourself out of the clutter and above your competition, this IS the work you will do—because I can promise you, they won't.

It's Going to Get Weird.
Embrace the Weirdness.

A lot of what you see and are told throughout this book, and that you'll discover if you begin collecting, accumulating, and studying major direct marketers' direct-mail and other marketing, will look, sound, or feel *wrong* to you. Too bold, too aggressive, too hype-y, too unprofessional, too weird, too contradictory to everything you see done in your field, too whatever. Of course, that's the old you reacting to it, before you became a knowledgeable direct-marketing pro. Regardless, your opinions *never* count. You don't get a vote, because you don't put money into your cash register. Your spouse, momma, neighbor, golfing buddy, competitor, or employees don't get to vote either, for the same reason—and you must explain to them, in no uncertain terms, that they have no vote. The clout belongs exclusively to the customer. The only votes that get counted are the customers', and the only legal, valid ballots are cash, checks, and credit cards. Everything else is B.S.

With this Rule #9 to live by, you will be the most results-oriented businessperson on the planet, immune to opinion, criticism, or guesswork. If it sells, it's good. If it doesn't, it isn't. You are going to quickly become "Mr. or Mrs. or Miss Money-in-the Bank." If you can't clearly track money in the bank from something, stop doing it. There's likely an EXIT sign above a door in your place of business. Through that door goes anything and everything (and anyone) not definitively putting money in the bank. And if something that does put money in the bank is "weird," so be it.

Tim Ferris told me he chose his first book's title, *The Four-Hour Workweek*, by testing many possible titles via Google AdWords, and that the winning title was not his preferred choice. He let the market choose. His book soared to bestseller status and made him famous and rich. Personally, I detest the book's title and abhor the idea people get from it. But I admire Tim's wisdom in counting the right votes.

I had a client with upscale home furnishings stores who suffered a wife thoroughly embarrassed by his personality-driven, inelegant direct-mail campaigns. Every year he spent a good-sized sum producing a fancy, slick, prestigious brochure about his stores that he never actually used. The entire exercise was to give his wife something she was willing to let her family and friends see, that represented their business! Many people have echoed her level of distress to me about using direct-response advertising—until they saw and banked the results.

To be a committed direct marketer, you must be committed to *results*.

The world, incidentally, is overrun with people claiming desire for all sorts of results—from wealth to weight loss—but unwilling to do what is required to achieve the results, even when that requirement is clear and within their doing. That is a fundamental difference between the few winners and the bulk of losers in every endeavor: The winners prize the desired result above every other consideration and are willing to do whatever it takes (within the law) to get that result. The losers think and say they want the result, but they want it only if they can have it somehow gifted to them, without meeting its requirements.

When it comes to driving a business to exceptional heights, an income to the top 5% or 1%, a product to dominance in the marketplace, there are known requirements—almost always including violating industry norms, being judged odd and being roundly criticized, setting aside all opinions, and relentlessly focusing on what works.

If you narrow this, and return from it as broad principle to micro-marketing strategy, you will arrive at a requirement for commitment to Direct Marketing and Direct-Response Advertising. I have made an admittedly informal but, I think, fair and fairly comprehensive study of the startups in all fields that have grown to make their owners rich, and the ratio of those using Direct Marketing vs. those using other types of marketing is about 50 to 1. As an investor, if a company is not heavily utilizing Direct Marketing and Direct-Response Advertising, I'm nervous about owning stock in it, and rarely do. Although he has never enunciated it, an examination of Warren Buffett's investing reveals the same bias. Conversely, there's a big graveyard of companies begun and built with direct marketing, sold to and bought by much bigger "normal" companies, and quickly destroyed and bankrupted. These failures all involve confusion and mixed agendas and loss of focus on what produces results.

Beware
New Metrics Nonsense

You will be told that you can't measure new media with old metrics. That trying to hold social media like Facebook or YouTube accountable, in hard dollars and cents, to the same direct return on investment terms as you can print, direct-mail, and broadcast advertising is unreasonable and antiquated thinking. The best answer I've heard for this, from an employer to several members of his marketing team: "Fine. As long as I can write new metrics instead of dollars on *your* paycheck, I'll let you spend my marketing resources on new metrics."

Anytime anyone or anything seeks to hide from precise accountability, there's B.S. in the air. Beware!

I have watched the marketing world invaded by 20- and 30-year-olds pushing their employers and clients to invest untold sums and resources in online and social media that they claim defies measurement yet is both essential and effective,

---

Beware: New Metrics Nonsense, cont.

and get away with it, because they speak an invented language, a new media gibberish, that confuses and intimidates their senior bosses. This is mysticism. It is not new. It is as old as the Ouija Board, as old as wizards enriched by kings. I am writing this book in my 40th anniversary year in advertising and marketing, and I have seen this same mysticism before. Many current practitioners think it is new. It is not. It is a rerun. There are always mystics inventing new ways to conceal perfidy.

In the trade journals read by the Direct Marketing industry, articles by mystics pronouncing old media and old metrics dead and promoting their preferred, unaccountable, new media abound. But in the real world, where money is actually made with marketing by people who must account for their dollars—small business—a very different viewpoint grows by the day. Here's what one of our successful GKIC Members*, John Melley, wrote about his own conclusion: "I've also decided that Facebook is a gigantic, narcissistic time suck. Yes, I too got caught up in this 'shiny object' and wasted time and money trying to harness it. My time and efforts are spent better elsewhere. Others say I'm missing the boat, but every dime I've made this year was made outside Facebook." (JohnMelley.com)

Ryan Holiday, the Marketing Director for the trendy American Apparel Company, has provided a remarkably candid exposé of online blogs in his book *Trust Me, I'm Lying: Confessions of a Media Manipulator*, that reveals how blogging as a business

---

*Mr. Melley is one of tens of thousands of Members of GKIC, the international organization for marketing-oriented entrepreneurs and business owners. Information about a free offer from GKIC appears on page 175.

Beware: New Metrics Nonsense, cont.

and as a means of promoting businesses, people, and causes really works—and it is very grimy and ugly, enormously time-consuming far beyond what most businesspeople can give it, and can best be described from a marketing standpoint as *very indirect* marketing. An in-depth article in *The Wall Street Journal* (October 8, 2012) discussed online/social media from Facebook to BuzzFeed, but in the entire report, could not cite one dollars-and-cents outcome, instead talking the new language of viral video, visits, views, etc. Maybe most radically, in B. J. Mendelson's book, *Social Media Is Bullshit*, premiered in 2012, he asserted, "None of these social media platforms are good for business . . . Offline matters more than online . . . Be skeptical of metrics like 'awareness' and 'engagement'—these and other new social media metrics don't mean anything." Because you hear so much about online and social media and are under such pressure to invest time and money in more and more of it, I urge reading both these books to hear a couple of very different perspectives.

I May Sometimes Be Mistaken For The Angry Old Man Yelling At Kids To Get Off His Lawn, But . . .

To paraphrase a famous line, I don't "give 'em hell." I demand facts, and when they can't give them to me, they think it's hell. Marketing decisions can be made based on mysticism or based on facts and directly measurable monetary results, and you get to choose which seems most sensible and most likely to lead to success.

Beware: New Metrics Nonsense, cont.

I have a few big company clients—only a few, because my temperament is ill-suited for corporate bureaucracy and politics and foolishness, and I prefer clients with agility rather than size. But I have a few. Some have grown up from seedlings to gigantic empires with me over 10, 20, 30 years, like the Guthy-Renker Corporation, owner of direct-response TV created consumer product brands like Proactiv®, the $800 million-a-year acne treatment business. Others find me, perhaps as a result of a book like this, and bring me in to crack the direct-response whip.

In these places, I often find myself unwelcome when confronting the mystics ensconced in their conference rooms. They attempt, behind my back or openly, to characterize me as an angry elder being rendered irrelevant by dynamic change I do not understand. I suppose I aid their false characterization by well-known personal preferences: I *personally* refuse to use the internet, do not own a cell phone, and have a restored 1986 Jeep Wagoneer (with no GPS, no Facebook screen, no iPhone dock) as my everyday car.

However, in direct and intimate work with clients and on my own projects, I drive online sales in excess of $100 million a year—with websites, online video, online sales letters, online catalogs, even social media, and, predominately, offline media directing traffic to online sales points, and, beyond that, more loosely connected to me, online sales exceeding $2.5 billion occur annually. It is a completely false conceit to marginalize me or to seek escape from my sharp-eyed scrutiny and sharp-tongued critique. I am certainly NOT going to tell you that online and/or social media can't be deployed profitably or even advise you to risk abstaining from at least some of it. A website, for example, is nearly an essential, and if you're going to have one, several, or many,

Beware: New Metrics Nonsense, cont.

you might as well have fully functional Direct Marketing sites. But I am going to stridently caution you against pursuing the new and exotic and seemingly cheap media if not even making full use of the most reliable, directly measurable, and profitable investments you can make.

I can't bear to watch baseball, because there are only two people working most of the time, with everybody else standing around scratching themselves and watching. I started out poor and I've been scrounge-in-the-car-seat-cushions-for-change-for-dinner broke. The kid with the MBA in marketing, bought and paid for by his parents and government-subsidized debt, who has arrived in your office all dewy and fresh and in love with new media and new metrics has never had to sweat blood over a dollar. I have. You probably have—and don't forget it. Don't let anybody bamboozle you with bullshit into letting dollars play or stand around or escape the mandate to measurably multiply. Your motto must be: *If it doesn't pay, not today.*

It's okay <u>not</u> to be cool or first or early. There are a lot of tested, proven, formulaic and reliable marketing methods and media to use to grow a business. A lot. And real estate on the internet is inexhaustible. You can't be locked out anywhere by coming late, nor can you take a hill and hold it by getting there first. You can wait and stubbornly insist on waiting to put money into a slot until there's a certainty of getting money back out.

A Story

Many years ago, I found myself in Nassau, with nearly empty pockets. Less than a hundred dollars and days ahead of me.

Beware: New Metrics Nonsense, cont.

I dressed up nice and went to the big casino then over the bridge on Paradise Island—now replaced by Atlantis. I stood behind players at the roulette table and, with painful patience, waited until either red or black or odd or even, just red, or just black, or just odd, or just even had failed to hit five times in a row. This doesn't happen much, so I stood there for 20, 30, 40 minutes at a time without placing a bet. But when it happened, I bet on the one that had not come up five times in a row. If I lost, I doubled my bet. And doubled again. (There is risk of wipe-out, as there's a 0 and double-00 to contend with, but I never wiped out.) I ever so slowly, ever so tediously, very methodically built my little bankroll up. When chased away from the roulette table, I wandered over to the Wheel of Fortune, where you bet on whether the $1 bill, $5 bill, $10 bill, $20 bill, $50 bill, or $100 bill will come up—with commensurate payoff: 1–1 if the $1, 5–1 if the $5, etc. There are a lot more $1 spots than anything else on the wheel. Again, I waited for long spans until five consecutive spins failed to land on the $1. Then I swooped and started. In almost 9 hours, I grew my stash from its dangerous start of $100.00 to almost $1,200.00.

I don't recommend it—it's more pain than play, and you suffer the evil eye of dealers and pit bosses, and you could lose everything even with this conservative a scheme. I'm not dispensing gambling advice here. I am pointing out a couple of things. If you truly prize your dollars and seek to squander nary one, there are very reliable ways to put them to work, in marketing, or even at the casino. You can take care to put them where their odds favor you substantially.

Also, many years ago now, I got to know one of the rare, consistently successful and quietly rich professional blackjack

Beware: New Metrics Nonsense, cont.

players who "went public" fairly late in his career, to write about and teach highest probability play, a man named Jerry Patterson. Jerry said that 99% of all gamblers succumb to mysticism and magic. They believe they can "feel" a streak coming on, that there are certain machines in a casino subject to paying off much more generously than others, that feng shui may apply, that wearing their lucky socks or sitting between a blonde and a redhead or getting a room on the 7th or 11th floor, or only sitting down at a blackjack table after the dealer has busted matters. Jerry said, *"You can trust magic. Or you can trust math. I prefer math."* Winning at blackjack, for the very few who do and are permitted to keep playing, is all about deep understanding of the mathematical probabilities, somehow counting at least to rich or poor in high cards even with multiple decks, patience, and grinding out small profits over time.

Math or Magic?

All the math your accountant won't give you and they don't teach those dewy MBAs in business school that is critical for you to know and run your business with is presented in Chapter 43 of my book, *No B.S. Ruthless Management of People and Profits*. It's possibly my most powerful and least popular book. Note the word: ruthless.

A biggie is <u>direct</u> ROI.

Elsewhere in this book, I acknowledge the influence, power, and value of brand. Yet I am fervently opposed to brand-building advertising or marketing. I believe you build brand free as a byproduct of direct response.

Beware: New Metrics Nonsense, *cont.*

See Chapter 4 for more. So, yes, there are many indirect pay-offs and intangible benefits that accrue from aggressive, effective advertising, marketing, and promotion that combine to rising tide. Brand is one. Discouragement or even barrier to competition, another. Price elasticity, another (as the better known entity tends to be the more easily trusted entity, and trust plays a major role in price**). However, it is my game plan to buy none of this, not to try and count it at all, as it is fundamentally uncountable. And I urge you not to fall into paying for the new and mystical metrics of numbers of likes, friends, page views, minutes spent at site or page, or anything of the sort. You can pay *attention* to it. Just *don't pay money* for it.

When anybody wants you to pay for what can't be counted in dollars directly returned, remember your mantra: *If it doesn't pay, not today.*

A big differentiator between true-blue direct marketers—a fraternity this book is trying to bring you into—and all other marketers is: direct return on investment. Another, I would argue, is sensible, rational thinking versus stupidity. One of the most famous ad men of all time, a leader of the golden age (think: *Mad Men*), David Ogilvy, agreed with the latter. He famously told his agency folk, in a blustery tirade prompted by expressed mysticism, that, quote, "Only the direct-response people really know what the hell they are doing."

**For a comprehensive look at trust, refer to my book *No B.S. Guide to Trust-Based Marketing*.

CHAPTER 9

No Chocolate Cake for You!

*S*einfeld's creation, The Soup Nazi, is a memorable character. The proprietor of a soup shop, he tells anyone who annoys him, "No soup for you!" If you're going to get very far with this conversion to Direct Marketing, you're going to have to yell at yourself and deny yourself things you've been indulging in. By the time you finish this book, you'll have seen the prior nine rules applied and been directed to a number of places where you can see them applied. What may have started out as mysterious will be understood. You'll be able to spot Direct Marketing when you see it. You'll know what needs to be done. The real question left will be about your will to do what you know needs to be done.

Rule #10
You Will Be A Tough-Minded Disciplinarian and Put Your Business on a Strict Direct Marketing Diet

Business success is about iron will in many ways. Many business owners who perennially struggle and suffer are very much aware of things that need doing but simply lack the will to do them. There's a longtime employee or vendor or client, now a "friend," who you know is toxic and detrimental and needs to be replaced, but you can't muster the will to fire them. There's advertising you keep spending money on that you know is failing to produce measurable results, but you lack the will to end it or fix it. There's that website you know isn't producing, either, but the very thought of getting it remade (yet again) is painful, so it stays as-is. The will to win is found in winners and is often absent in also-rans.

If you go on a diet—*seriously*—there are some things you need to do. First, purge your refrigerator and cupboards of fattening and junk foods. And keep them free of them. Celery sticks, not cookies. Second, decide on an eating plan and stick to it patiently and persistently. Make it simple, with hard-and-fast rules you can remember. For example, not eating anything that's white is a very simple rule to remember. Third, get some tools, like a scale. Fourth, count something—calories, fat grams, carbs, Weight Watchers points, *something*—so you can manage with numbers. Fifth, step up your exercise. Finally, sixth, be very alert to hazards and scams that lead you astray. An example, a friend recently proudly showed me the bottle of "Vitamin Water" she had switched to from soda pop to be healthier. The label on the small bottle of red gunk said it was a delivery system for *32 grams of sugar!* Gotta read the labels—if you're serious.

Same thing with your transformation to lean, mean, direct marketer.

First, purge your business of junk, like fancy brochures that violate most of the previous nine rules. Dead image or brand ads that just lay there. Gentle, subtle, plain vanilla sales letters. Media that can't be ruthlessly measured and held accountable. Uncooperative staff. Out with the old, in with the new. Not slowly or gradually, either. Just like with the refrigerator and pantry—get a big trash bag and purge. The great success philosopher, colleague, and friend of mine, Jim Rohn, was known far and wide for preaching the gospel of Massive Action. Key word: *massive*. Jim McCann, founder of 1-800-Flowers, who appeared on several programs with me, including one of our own GKIC Marketing & Moneymaking SuperConferences℠, talked about having to open the door of his marketing department and throw in a bomb now and then, to blow everything up, destroy all assumptions and habits, and start anew. This is what I want this book to inspire you to do, and give you the gumption to do: Blow it up, install Direct Marketing.

Second, decide on a new marketing plan. Like the eating plan, it's best if it is simple, with hard-and-fast rules that are easy to remember. Rules #2, #3, and #4 on previous pages are just as clear, simple, and easily kept in mind as Eat Nothing White. I suggest my book *The Ultimate Marketing Plan (4th Edition)* as a good guide to creating your own simple and straightforward marketing plan. You *do* need a written plan. Organized effort.

Third, get some good tools. New ads, fliers, sales letters, websites, email follow-up sequences, scripts for handling incoming calls, maybe marketing system software like Infusionsoft, which powers GKIC, most of my clients' businesses, I recommend. A very simple, easy-to-follow guide is my book *The Ultimate Sales Letter (4th Edition)*. A more robust tool kit including templates and ready-to-use marketing documents is my *Magnetic Marketing System* (DanKennedy. com/Store). A list of basic Direct Marketing tools required by just about any business appears at the end of this chapter. It's said that a poor carpenter blames his tools, and I suppose that's true, but the flip is true, too: Poor tools make it difficult to be a good carpenter.

If you are going to very seriously tackle everything discussed here, convert yours to a Direct Marketing business, implement thorough follow-up, and fully monetize every lead and customer, you are probably going to want and need to automate your marketing system. To that end, I have a crass commercial recommendation for Infusionsoft. GKIC's own marketing, a goodly number of my private clients' businesses, and many GKIC Members' businesses are powered by Infusionsoft. It succeeds where other CRM or sales software fails, because it was designed in the first place by and for Direct Marketers, and for owners of Non-Direct Marketing Businesses converting to Direct Marketing. It is endorsed by America's #1 small-business systemization guru, Michael Gerber, author of *The E-Myth*. Figure 9.1 shows you a B2B'er, an industrial equipment and services marketer, Walter Bergeron's report on the impact of Infusionsoft— and the kind of marketing you're discovering here—on his business. And you can learn more and get a demonstration at GKICLovesInfusionsoft.com. In the interest of transparency, I am a stockholder in Infusionsoft, but I did that after we first utilized it, after I judged it the best system for implementing Direct Marketing at the small-business level. The company is a client of mine as well. Again, if you are going to seriously tackle everything in this book, I recommend investigating how this one-of-a-kind tool can help you.

FIGURE 9.1: Walter Bergeron's Report

Reprinted from the *No B.S. Marketing Letter,* October 2012

EXPOSED! "THE UNFAIR ADVANTAGE MARKETING JUGGERNAUT

(Hint: It involves more than simply doing things just like everyone else.)

My name is **Walter Bergeron** and I run Power Control Services Inc, located in Broussard, Louisiana. I started this company 16 years ago in the middle of the sugarcane fields in Louisiana after I finished 6 years in the US Navy, where they taught me how to repair nuclear power plant electronics. (And yes I do glow in the dark!)

Our primary business is the repair of industrial electronic circuit boards.

For example, one of our clients is Tyson foods and you probably know they produce ready to cook poultry products. What you might not realize is they have an entire manufacturing process involving conveyor belts and metal detectors and all sorts of electronic automation equipment. Very often, that equipment breaks down for various reasons and we are the company they call when they need it fixed.

"My Marketing Strategy? Do What Everyone Else Was Doing..."

Now even if you haven't heard of my business or type of business before, trust me, we're not unique. We have plenty of competition and my marketing strategy historically had been pretty much to do what everyone else was doing. (Sound familiar?)

What that meant was we would hire an advertising agency to help us generate our marketing materials. They were all very pretty and shiny and sparkly but frankly did not produce huge numbers in terms of actual sales.

We also did what everyone else in our industry was doing by hiring outside sales staff and making sales calls, taking prospects to lunch, and basically doing lots of one to one selling. It was mildly effective and resulted in a steady, but slow, growth.

The Power of GKIC Marketing and Infusionsoft Changed Everything!

Around 2010, I began to dabble in the GKIC style of marketing when I bought Dan's "Magnetic Marketing" system and also joined as a Gold Member. I definitely resonated with everything I was hearing from GKIC and Dan Kennedy. I loved the ideas, but frankly, I never managed to get around to actually implementing anything of any real significance.

Something always prevented me. I was always in search for the next new shiny object that would get me where I wanted to go.

Then in September 2011, after attending GKIC's Fast Implementation Bootcamp, I finally decided to dedicate myself to 90 days of MASSIVE Action. I implemented multiple strategies simultaneously: I updated my newsletter, developed a multi-step direct mail campaign, segmented my customer list into much clearer distinctions, and several other items as well.

I'd heard about Infusionsoft while listening to a GKIC monthly CD in my car. The guy mentioned automating our marketing process and talked about Infusion. I didn't know what he was talking about, so I did a little Google search and a phone call later, we were up and running on Infusionsoft.

Now I'll admit, I was fearful that the monthly investment would be a waste of money because it couldn't possibly perform up to the same level as our very high end, costly, in-house software.

Well, *I was oh so very wrong!*

Superior Ideas Require Superior Systems

I wouldn't be telling you this story unless I made the major shift from our old, outdated software to Infusionsoft.

Before Infusionsoft, we used internal software that was integrated into our Enterprise Resource Planning (ERP) system – software that controls the entire business from accounting to production to payroll.

The challenge with that system was it was very hard to use and so slow and cumbersome! We would work for 4 plus hours to create a single email and we had to do that each and every time; automation or customization was not possible.

We wanted software that would make creating marketing pieces easy and automated, but we had no idea of the power we unleashed with Infusionsoft.

We discovered that we could use the power of Infusionsoft for many other media such as faxes, direct mail, tasks and internal correspondence. Now we even use Infusionsoft in our production department for reminders about deadlines and events.

Can You Say "Cha-ching" Baby!?

With Infusionsoft we're able to take the ideas from GKIC to create powerful, multi-step campaigns – "Unfair Advantage Marketing Juggernauts" – that have radically transformed my business and its revenues.

In fact, we produced $1,120,197.77 in just 90 days of implementing GKIC marketing, using Infusionsoft as the backbone of the campaigns.

By using the marketing content and leveraging GKIC techniques in concert with Infusionsoft we've been able to craft complex and completely unfair campaigns involving emails, faxes, phones, shock and awe packages!

I have launched my business to a whole new level that would never have been possible had I only done one or the other.

The synergistic effect of combining these two dynamo companies has enabled my company to establish and maintain a completely unfair advantage over my competitors.

I strongly urge you to give yourself that same unfair advantage by partnering with Infusionsoft today:

http://www.GKICLovesInfusionsoft.com

Fourth, start counting and measuring things. Closely monitor numbers that matter.

Let me share a story shared with me by a Disney Imagineer. If you visit Disney World, you will see kids engaging in pin-trading with employees. I'm told they monitor, track, and analyze each pin-trading employee's productivity by pins sold at the locations they're stationed at, hour by hour, day by day, in like weather conditions, etc., etc., to constantly make decisions about which employees should be trading and which shouldn't, where and when. Secretly, Disney may be The Most Micro-Managed Place on Earth.

If you don't come up with things you can count and measure by hour, day, week, month, and ways to hold your every dollar invested directly accountable, your attempt at conversion from ordinary marketing to Direct Marketing will fail. For a complete dissertation of "money math" and the numbers that matter, consult my book *No B.S. Ruthless Management of People and Profits*. I also urge reading Michael Levine's book *Broken Windows, Broken Business*, a short, un-sweet management guide, based in part on the tactics that Rudy Guiliani used to transform New York City from unsafe to safe, from dirty to clean.

Fifth, step up your exercise to build your marketing mind muscle. Throughout this book, I recommend other books; my own and others'. If you're like most business owners, you get completely caught up in the "doing of things," to such extent you aren't actually thinking much, let alone considering new and different and potentially better ways of growing your business. These days, this has escalated to new mental illness, as people have removed even the minutes of walks from business to car or with the dog from thinking time to cell-phone calling and texting and email checking and Facebook updating time. I suggest at least one hour first thing in the morning and one hour in the evening given to reading success literature and marketing information, and making notes and working on changes and improvements in your business. Further, you need to actually become your business's chief marketing officer and devote a significant amount of time just to marketing work. I get professional practice owners to force all their appointments into four days and block one day a week to do marketing work and only marketing work. You also need to mentally exercise and build marketing mind muscle by association with other businesspeople committed to Direct Marketing, in your category of products and services if possible, or/ and in diverse businesses. One path to such associations on a national and local level is through GKIC, starting at the gateway offer on page 175.

Sixth, finally, be alert for and resistant to those who would dissuade or distract you from putting your business on the Direct Marketing Diet. You need to be very careful not to let anything into your new Direct Marketing business that doesn't belong there. Consider the bread the restaurant gives me with my salad. When I get a big Caesar salad with grilled chicken from a nearby restaurant as take-out, they always put one-third of a loaf of fresh-baked bread in with it. When I get home, I take the bread out of its wrapper and throw it in the big garbage can in the garage before entering the house. Why? Because I have a lot less discipline than most people give me credit for. If that bread gets past the perimeter into my house, I'll eat it. So I can't let it in. You've got to do the same thing with your business. Anything that doesn't conform to the Rules here, do not let in at all. Just say no. And bar the door.

BASIC Direct Marketing Tools List

Front-End/New Customer Acquisition

- *Lead-Generation Magnets*: books, reports, CDs, online videos, etc., that offer information of prime interest to your desired customers, clients, or patients, that can be advertised and promoted, and when delivered, establish your authority, credibility, expertise, trusted advisor status, and promote your products, services, and business.
- *Website(s)* that capture visitors' contact information for follow-up and present your information.
- *Main (Long-Form) Sales Letter(s)* that sell the core product/service or the sale-event, i.e., appointment, in-store visit, etc.
- *Follow-Up System for Unconverted Leads*: online and offline steps, put into a sequence.
- *In-Bound Call Script* that includes capture of prospects' contact information for follow-up.

Back-End/Customer Retention, Ascension, Repeat Business Nurture, Referrals Nurture

- Online/Offline Sequences for each sales purpose—for example, cross-selling the buyer of Item #A into Item #B.
- Seasonal/Holiday Promotions.
- Customer Newsletter or alternative, regularly delivered goodwill/relationship-nurturing material.
- Referral stimulation campaign(s).
- Late or Lost Customer Re-Activation campaign.
- Catalog, offline and/or online, of all goods and services.

For more detailed information about these tools and referral to relevant resources, access the Special Report: Direct Marketing Tool-Kit at www.NoBSBooks.com/Direct MarketingBook.

CHAPTER 10

The Results Triangle

E very marketing system I've ever devised for any client—and they now number in the hundreds and hundreds, commanding fees exceeding $100,000.00 plus royalties—every one has been based on the Message-Market-Media Triangle. It is not, therefore, unique to this book. I teach it elsewhere, often, and rely on it as I do gravity and oxygen.

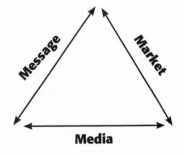

Message-Market-Media

There are basically three components to marketing, for anything, anywhere,

at any price, to anyone. Every individual loves to insist his business circumstances are somehow different. Not so. Every business, past or present, requires these three things to prosper: a Marketing Message, a Media to deliver it, and a Market to receive and respond to it. These three cannot be placed in any certain sequential order, because any one is no more important than the other, and none can function without the others. It is a closed triangle. Each feeds the others. If you will, "marketing energy" flows to and from each component, from each one to the other two.

There are a number of ways to render the Triangle powerless:

1. Right Message—Wrong Market—Right Media
2. Right Message—Right Market—Wrong Media
3. Right Message—Wrong Market—Wrong Media
4. Wrong Message—Right Market—Right Media
5. Wrong Message—Wrong Market—Right Media
6. Wrong Message—Right Market—Wrong Media
7. Wrong Message—Wrong Market—Wrong Media (the trifecta)

There's only one way to get it right.

Right Message—Right Market—Right Media

Now let's look at getting all three parts functioning effectively and in sync with the others.

Markets
How to Discriminate for Fun and Profit!

With a nod to Dr. Seuss, the WHO is very, very important.

When you choose and use Media, it's vital to know WHO you are trying to reach, attract, interest and persuade, and how they prefer to be offered and receive information and offers. When you craft your Message, you need to know WHO it is for (and WHO it isn't). The WHO you want as a customer gets to govern everything.

If you re-read that paragraph, you'll think it all obvious. Yet, most marketing remains product-centric, not customer-centric, and most marketing is very broad and vague and generic, not narrow, focused, and specific. If you consider non-direct-response advertising, i.e., image or brand advertising, its emphasis is on the company and the brand, not about the customer.

Most small businesses attempt to influence the ocean with thimbles-full of water. When you have comparatively limited resources, you must deploy them very selectively.

Sadly, most businesspeople cannot accurately and completely describe exactly WHO they want to respond, WHO is their ideal customer, WHO is their current customer, and for the most part they are playing Blind Archery. A dangerous game.

I have dealt with many, many, many examples of this over the years. Let me tell you about three that are instructive and, in very, very different businesses, reveal the same very powerful, profitable, pretty much secret principle.

Scenario #1: A member of one of my coaching groups owned a very profitable, very unusual business: For a fee, his company helped frustrated U.S. men meet and marry brides from foreign countries and arrange for their immigration. His was a one-stop shop, providing access to thousands of women in Russia, Asia, and other lands eager to marry U.S. men, who had been pre-screened. The company facilitated communication, coaching, trips to the different countries, and assistance with legal matters. The basic fees were $495.00 to $995.00 when he joined my group, but they quickly leapt to

$4,995.00 to $9,995.00 on my advice, with no change in client acceptance, although that's not my point here. I questioned him about the WHO of his business. Who were the clients? Who were the *best* clients? He told me they were everybody: preachers, teachers, truck drivers, pro golfers, executives, barbers, butchers, and candlestick makers. But when I asked if there were more of one than the other, I hit the nerve; he didn't know. So we investigated. And we found that about half of all the clients were twice-divorced, long-haul truck drivers. Now I want you to think about what use we might make of that piece of information, and we'll return to it a bit later.

Scenario #2: A client sold a homebased business opportunity aimed at "white collar" men and women. He advertised in *USA TODAY,* newspapers, and business-opportunity-type magazines, like this book's publisher's magazine, *Entrepreneur.* Again, I inquired about the WHO. His buyers included "all kinds of" sales professionals, accountants, lawyers, doctors, executives, and retired persons. But when I asked if there were more of one than the other, he wasn't sure. We investigated. Over one-third were accountants and CPAs, about one-third mortgage brokers, and the remaining one-third a mixed bag. Now I want you to think about what use we might make of that piece of information, and we'll return to it a bit later.

Scenario #3: I was doing a lot of work with a particular chiropractor, and we meticulously analyzed his records and surveyed his patients to discover the majority of his fee-for-service cash patients had two things in common: One, they paid using their American Express cards, rather than VISA or MasterCard, and two, they subscribed to *Prevention* magazine. The majority. Now I want you to think about what use we might make of that piece of information, and we'll return to it a bit later.

Go back to the first example, the foreign brides business. With the information uncovered, here's what he could do: First, radically alter the places he advertised and the amounts of money allocated to different places. There are magazines for and read only by truck drivers, truck stops where literature can be distributed, mailing lists. So instead of spending 100% of the ad dollars in general media like *USA TODAY*, at least half could go where half the clients are coming from. In the Kennedy Marketing Triangle, I've just addressed Media. Second, he could take all his generic ads, sales letters, testimonial booklets, etc., and tweak them, creating a version talking only to and about truck drivers, featuring only testimonials from truck drivers. In the Triangle, that's Message.

Consider the second example—obvious now, isn't it? There are magazines for and read only by accountants and CPAs, mailing lists, associations, meetings, and conferences. Same kind of Media change, same kind of Message change.

Now, the third example. In the commercial mailing-list marketplace, you can rent the list of *Prevention* magazine subscribers by ZIP code (as well as by gender, age, etc.) and you can rent the list of American Express cardholders by ZIP code. He took only the duplicates, the people in his market area on both lists. Because he had to rent 5,000 names from each list as a required minimum, it cost him about $700.00, and he only found 27 prime names in his area—a cost to find them of about $26.00 each. A lot of business owners would scream, "Too much money!" Dumb, dumb, dumb. How much do you think it will cost running ordinary ads or mass mailing neighborhoods to find 27 who precisely and perfectly match your ideal customer profile? From sequential mailings to the 27, he got 11 into the office (40% response!—vs. 1% or 2% norm from mass mail); 9 became patients, producing

$17,800.00 in immediate revenue, plus long-term value, plus referrals. That's the potential power of laser-beam-targeted marketing.

All three scenarios teach the same lessons. The WHO is very, very important. If you know WHO you want to attract, you can often find media or lists that reach only them. Often, the right description of WHO already exists in your business and you just haven't paid any attention to it or thought about how to use it.

Well, what if you're new in business and have no backlog of data about your WHO? Try common sense. Maybe check your trade association or even competitors for some clues to WHO. A client of mine starting a brand-new, high-end, gourmet food and wine store camped out in a competing store's parking lot and a nearby top-price restaurant's parking lot, stick counted make and model of cars, and found a profound bias for new and nearly new *foreign* luxury cars, so he rented lists of those car owners in his ZIP code. Or, at least, start out with your own preferences. WHO do you want as client or customer? One way or another, get out of the anybody 'n' everybody place at your earliest opportunity.

Personally, I long ago discovered that my best clients, best coaching group members, and highest value customers were politically conservative males from everywhere but the East Coast "blue states." Are there exceptions? Yes, and in sizable numbers—I have and have had great women clients, a few flaming liberal clients, and very good clients from New York. But the majority, conservative males, mostly from the Midwest, South, and Southwest. Consequently, I make no attempt to be all-inclusive in what I write, say, or produce, nor do I give even a minute's thought to whom I might offend in the lower value, lower percentage groups. I know my prime Market and I design my Messages and choose my Media accordingly.

At bare minimum, let this chapter make you think more about Markets. Too many businesspeople think about themselves, their products, their services, and what they want to say about all that, rather than thinking about WHO is likely to be hungriest, most eager, most receptive, is readily and affordably reachable, that they'll enjoy doing business with.

Let me be VERY clear: As long as you refuse to dig in and become sophisticated and smart about selection, discrimination, and target marketing so as to clone and attract ideal customers, clients, or patients, there are three bad things that will remain true for you: 1) you will be conforming to what the majority of average businesspeople do, therefore 2) you will be prohibited from rising above the average income the majority of businesspeople earn, therefore 3) you will be unprotected from and perennially vulnerable to commoditization, competition, and income disruption by recession or other adverse circumstances.

What I have described to you here in this introduction to list selection and target marketing is not simple, but it's not impossibly complicated, either; it's not easy, but it's not impossibly hard, either. If a guy in the business of finding foreign brides, if a marketer of a business opportunity, if the owner of a local brick-and-mortar service business like a chiropractic practice can figure out how to identify and then directly aim at and attract their ideal customers, so can you.

You can move on to be even more sophisticated at this, too. At the end of this chapter, you'll get insight into that, in an exclusive discussion with me and Richard Seppala, one of the most sophisticated providers of data-mining expertise, consulting, and services in the country today.

I know, you feel too busy just running your business as you do now to try and become expert in something as foreign to you as data mining and list selection. I know, you feel your business may be too small and your income may be too small for you to afford to invest in high-value lists. You must understand that this is exactly how average businesspeople forever anchored to, at best, average incomes feel. There's no genius or real value in citing the 516 reasons you *can't*.

Message
How to Speak Magnetically to Your Chosen Market

You put out Marketing Messages constantly—whether you're fully conscious about it or not. People ask you, "What do you do?" and you answer them. You spend money advertising your business. You communicate with current customers. It's important to understand five things about all this communication:

1. Your customers and prospects are just buried in communication from your competitors and from countless others competing for their attention, if not their money.
2. Most communication intended to interest customers fails miserably.
3. Communication about products and services, about what you want to sell, are generally a lot more interesting to you than to your customers and would-be customers.
4. People are most interested in what interests them.
5. People are most easily and quickly interested in *information* directly related to what interests them—especially information that promises fascinating secrets, solutions to problems, prevention for dire threats, promises of seductive benefits, or timely "breaking news."

Item 5 is the breakthrough prescription for magnetic communication.

A good way to think about information you may create and offer is as bait. And a key principle is: MATCH BAIT TO CRITTER.

If you want a yard full of deer, do not put a 50-pound block of cheddar cheese outside. Put out a big salt block. If you want rats and mice, try the cheese. If you want to catch trout, do not tie an old shoe to your fishing line. Very simple formula.

Once you pick the critter you want to attract, as we just discussed in the previous chapter, you can then pick or create the right bait. In marketing, "bait" means two things: your Message and whatever "thing" you offer to spark direct response, whether that's literature and information, a free service, or a gift of one kind or another.

Most businesspeople get poor results from their advertising and marketing because they either put out no bait, lousy bait, or the wrong bait for the critters they hope to attract.

No bait, that's ordinary image or brand advertising, rather than direct response advertising.

Lousy bait is boring, uninteresting, unappealing bait. A free report on *"How to Buy Insurance"* is lousy bait. A free report on "How to Legally Avoid all Estate Taxes" might be better bait—for the right critter. That free report combined with a free audio CD with an interview with five wealthy executives about tax planning mistakes they were making and how they fixed them, and another free report, "How to Double Tax Free Yield On IRA, SEP, Keogh & Other Retirement Funds," makes for better bait.

Wrong bait for wrong critters—the free report on estate taxes, if you want to attract young married couples.

Sure, this (now) seems incredibly obvious and elementary. Yet 90% of all advertising features one of these three bait mistakes.

Then, there's a bigger issue this bait thing fits in. It's called Message-to-Market Match (or mismatch). Most business marketing is generic, one size fits all. Most marketing is done with generic tools: one brochure, one catalog, one website for everybody. But one size never fits all. What's magnetic is a Message just for me! As soon as I see it, I jump out of my skin because it is clearly for me, about me, matches me and my pain, fear, passion, hopes.

Media
How to Deliver a Magnetic Message to Your Chosen Audience

The list of media choices is longer than all the pages of this book ripped apart and laid end to end.

There are newspapers, magazines, freestanding inserts, TV, radio, coupons, postcards, fliers, sales letters, catalogs, websites, email, faxes, telemarketing, billboards, vehicle signs, bus bench signs, skywriting, package inserts, imprinted golf tees, website addresses tattooed on boxers' heads or strippers' body parts, and thousands of variations and other choices. Online, there's another entire collection of ever-expanding media. There are websites, online video, webinars, email, Facebook, Twitter, LinkedIn, YouTube, blogs, and more. And more. And more. What's good? What's bad? What's best? What's worst?

No simple answer. Sorry.

First, it varies a lot by business. But more importantly, it has to do with WHO you are trying to reach. Do they pay attention to and respond to the media? A flier for two-for-one pizza stuffed under windshield wipers of cars at a swap meet may be a good media. A flier about investing at least $250,000.00 in international currency funds stuffed under the same windshield wipers, bad media. But it's not the media. It's the use of it. The one sure thing is this: If the media can't be used to deliver a *direct response* message, skip it.

With that said, your mandate is to try to find ways to use as many different media as you possibly can. Most business owners become lazily dependent on only one, two, or three means of getting customers, leaving themselves vulnerable to sudden business disruption and entry of more aggressive competition.

Interview with Richard Seppala, The ROI Guy

Richard Seppala is a leading authority on data mining for direct marketing, what he refers to as cracking the DNA code of customer and prospect databases.

DAN KENNEDY: Let's begin with data mining. What is it?

RICHARD SEPPALA: Finding the pink elephant who drives a '57 Cadillac in Denmark. In other words, digging into a business's customer data and information to identify common characteristics, then using that information to locate clones of those customers in others' lists and in the marketplace in general.

DAN: Give us an example.

RICHARD: Everybody watched the 2012 election. Mitt Romney broke political fundraising records—and I'm not talking about those crazy Super Pacs where billionaires contributed. I'm

---

Interview with Richard Seppala, cont.

talking about his campaign's success getting ordinary Americans to open up their pocketbooks. According to an Associated Press report, August 24, 2012, Romney used a secret weapon: data mining, or what I call "Database DNA." The Romney campaign hired a very experienced firm to sift through donor and potential donor data—including what they bought, spent, even if and how often they went to church—to identify which were most likely to donate to Romney, and which were most affluent. This makes marketing more science than guesswork. Now, I've always been a numbers guy, even before I became "The ROI Guy." At the very start of my career, at a huge corporation I won't name here, I used tracking techniques and statistics to guide marketing decisions. Now my company teaches people how to use this science, and we provide data mining for better return on investment from marketing dollars, as a service to clients.

DAN: Why do you use the term "DNA" for this?

RICHARD: You are getting to the inner workings of a customer, so you know what behavior he is most likely to repeat, so you can isolate those most likely to buy from you. At the most sophisticated level, we utilize analysis by powerful computers of thousands of databases, including information about property tax records, charitable contributions, voter registration, families and children, credit accounts, and purchases. Database DNA puts this information through a process that yields both demographic and psychographic or behavioral information. By analyzing Database DNA, the Romney campaign found donors in traditionally Democrat strongholds like San Francisco—and brought in over $350,000.00 from just this one area, during several months in 2012.

Interview with Richard Seppala, cont.

DAN: This will instantly sound beyond the reach of most business owners. But I tell people that there are a lot of ways to clone customers. The more you know about yours, the better. You can access buyer and subscriber lists through SRDS.com, and find buyers nationally or in any geographic area that match up with yours in demographics; age, rank, serial number, but also in known interests and purchases, which indicate likelihood to again respond to offers in the same category. Business owners can also use data about their customers or best customers to make marketing content decisions—which photos should they use, what should we talk about. I was recently visiting with a client in finance who'd determined that nearly three-quarters of their customers owned yachts. This may lead them to lists—as you suggested, registration, license, tax information may be available. There are definitely magazine subscriber lists. But even in less targeted advertising or in marketing materials, that piece of information tells me to make sure there's a photo of people enjoying themselves on their yacht. A story about this client's voyage. So I'd say there are ways every business owner can make good use of data.

RICHARD: I put data mining to work for my wife's dental practice, so it definitely is available to small-business owners. I think it's important to understand how much data's available. Richard Leveille's a good example. For more than 20 years, he's been doing the research to pick locations for Smoothie King franchises. He traveled town-to-town, built thick books with facts and figures about every local market—facts and figures compiled from maps, phone books, public records. Smoothie King has 600 locations and continues to expand, but Richard no longer

Interview with Richard Seppala, cont.

has to spend days traveling and weeks researching, because the information he needs can be generated by data mining in about four minutes. Where does all the data come from? As I often hear you say, Dan, privacy in America is dead. It comes from every one of us. When we're on Facebook, shop online, use a Rewards Card at a store, use our credit cards, buy from a catalog, we leave a record. Data collection is going on behind every social media site, every website, every store. People have been startled, after searching for a particular piece of information or item online, to see an advertisement for that product or a related product appear on their web pages soon after. That's how fast and ingrained these systems are. It's a bit creepy, but it's the new reality.

DAN: Can you share a data-mining example that anybody could potentially benefit from?

RICHARD: A grocery store chain tracking its Rewards Card data discovered that when men bought diapers on Thursdays and Fridays, they also bought beer. How did they use that odd piece of information? It meant the store should always keep diapers and beer at full retail prices on Thursdays and Fridays, because these guys were coming to buy these weekend essentials, and would buy them no matter what. It also suggested putting promotional displays of beer near the diapers on Thursdays and Fridays. Without the data, I don't think anybody would think to look for a connection between diaper and beer sales. But this is exactly the kind of quirky connection that Database DNA will reveal.

DAN: So, as a practical matter, business owners can start by considering what data and buying pattern and customer information

Interview with Richard Seppala, cont.

they have available, and dig into it to look—manually—for any of these connections, then figure out how to use whatever they find. They can also begin collecting more data. If they have a business of some size, say several stores—not just one, they can get your firm's help doing the analysis. Let me ask you this: What's the biggest misconception about this?

RICHARD: People are told that their customer list or database is their gold mine. But for many, that's more bull than bullion. You certainly should be marketing aggressively into your own database. But that's just the bedrock foundation. If you can segment your list based on factual information and data, you can match offers and presentations to them and market much more effectively. To go back to your example, that financial expert could enclose a photo of people enjoying their yacht only with a promotion sent to his clients and prospects who actually own yachts; send a golf photo to those who play golf; etc. You know, there would likely be a boost to response.

But the big opportunity, where we step in, is using data about a business's customers to pinpoint and find more of those exact same customers. Finding new customers is the most expensive and difficult task most business owners face. Because the owner doesn't know who to market to, they go after everybody in ZIP codes or grouped by very basic criteria, with no reason to believe most are well-suited to be customers. With that kind of *saturation,* you need to be present a lot, waste a lot, be very patient. With *penetration*, you can reach out to fewer prospects, you have a greater likelihood of not only getting more customers, but better customers. The questions are pretty simple, actually. *What do the best customers of a business have in common?*

Interview with Richard Seppala, cont.

Were they mostly single or married, have kids or not, have high or low credit card usage? If we identify these traits, could we then find prospects to target who shared those traits? Would they prove to be "best customers" too? My wife's dental practice is a great case study . . .

DAN: I just want to make the point that most business owners never ask these kinds of questions. If pressed on this, most will just shrug and insist their customers are everybody, old, young, married, single, white-collar, blue-collar, etc.—and by being this lazy about collecting and either poring over data or getting data mining done for them, they stay stuck in time. I mean, their 10th year in business they're still getting new customers the same way they were the 1st year. No smarter.

RICHARD: Well, that's right. I also find that what business own-ers think about their customers is very often wrong. In my wife's case, I asked her to describe who she thought her best patients were and what they were like. She made what she thought was a good appraisal. Then I did the work. Not surprisingly, 80% of her income came from 20% of her patients. That led us to objectively analyzing the 20%. When I assembled the facts about these patients, my wife was shocked to find that her best patients were opposite of her ideas. We then took the compos-ite profile of her best patients and cross-referenced it against potential patients in the area. As The ROI Guy, I had and have access to 61 million records with demographic information. We found THOUSANDS of people who were strikingly similar to the "best patient profile." We divided these potential patients into three groups: Empty Nesters (older couples with kids grown and gone), Affluent Married Couples Without Children, and

Interview with Richard Seppala, cont.

Affluent Families. This way, we could go to the three groups with three different direct-mail and email campaigns, something you mentioned earlier. By creating and using this Database DNA, we were targeting consumers who spend 120 times what average consumers spend in certain categories, and doing "waste management" by eliminating 90% of the geographic area, homeowner list most would mail. The results from this campaign were outstanding. A lot of "normal" direct mail for dental practices pulls from .05% to 1%, 2% top results. We got 7%.

DAN: Richard, that's exactly the way it's supposed to be done! And I think it's going to get more and more important to approach potential new customers this way.

RICHARD: It's certainly not getting easier or less costly to acquire customers. People are growing more and more resistant to material that doesn't instantly, personally interest them. The pink elephant who drives a '57 Cadillac and lives in Sweden wants auto polish engineered to protect classic Cadillacs in Sweden winters—he doesn't want just car polish. And if you know your best customer is that pink elephant with a '57 Cadillac, we can find him. So, my company's business is all about two things: our Database DNA analysis and profiling services, and our ROI Matrix tracking and marketing services that help business owners and professional practice owners get precise and accurate measurement of ROI from different marketing campaigns and efforts.

DAN: The bottom line of all this is that every business owner becoming a Direct Marketer needs to collect and mine customer data and information, and find ways to use the information he

Interview with Richard Seppala, cont.

gets and biases and commonalities he uncovers—just as you've described.

Richard Seppala, known as "The ROI Guy," helps companies maximize profits by accurately measuring return on investment. By identifying strengths and weaknesses, engaging in sophisticated data mining, and using proprietary tools like his "ROI MATRIX" and all-in-one automated systems that track real-time and accumulating value of each lead and customer, The ROI Guy delivers dramatic profit improvement. Richard is regularly sought out by the media, including NBC, ABC, CBS, and Fox affiliates as well as *The Wall Street Journal*, and *USA Today*.

To learn more, and obtain free special reports, visit: www.YourROIGuy.com or call 1-800-647-1909.

CHAPTER 11

The Secret to Infinitely Higher Response

ou have probably, at some point in your life, read Dale Carnegie's classic book, *How to Win Friends and Influence People*. If not, you should. You may even be a graduate of The Dale Carnegie Program, as hundreds of thousands, maybe millions of people are. It is, by far, the most enduring and successful course on communication, influence, attraction, and persuasion, period.

The Dale Carnegie Secret on Steroids

The core of the Dale Carnegie program contains the simplest of truths: One, people are more interested in themselves than in anyone or anything else; two, people want to be valued, respected, treated as important and catered to; three, each person believes himself, his business, his situation, his needs to be unique, and is most responsive to someone who acknowledges that and is somehow well-matched or expert in that unique scenario.

When you move this to Direct Marketing, you can inject it with steroids and make it unbelievably powerful. And, as you'll see in this chapter's examples, you can gain incredible competitive advantage, because few business owners are willing to customize their presentations for different audiences. I call this The Secret of Message to Market Match. Few understand it; fewer are ever willing to utilize it.

Here, first, in Figure 11.1, I have reprinted four samples of relatively simple direct-response postcards used by Gordon Quinton, a GKIC Member in the property/casualty/commercial insurance business. You're not seeing both sides, you're not seeing everything, but you are seeing enough. Here are some of his reported return on investment statistics, using only the first year, direct value of the clients obtained (not including subsequent years' value or referrals):

Septic Contractors	$13.00 income for $1.00 spent/1,300% ROI
Optometrists	$3.00 to $1.00/300% ROI
Apt. Bldg. Owners	$7.00 to $1.00/700% ROI

I imagine business insurance is, pretty much, business insurance, but Gordon has made himself and what he offers precision-matched to each type of prospective client. The optometrists get an entirely different postcard than do the HVAC contractors, than do apartment building owners, etc. Gordon customizes the headline, the "compare rates"

FIGURE 11.1: Gordon Quinton Example

Reprinted from the *No B.S. Marketing Letter,* October 2012

examples, photos, testimonials, even his own business's domain name for each niche. And there is further congruent customization, as he has a separate and different website for each niche, too. Hopefully, you instantly grasp how very different this is from most business insurance brokers' and agents' marketing; typically, one big, broad, sloppy and therefore uninteresting and ordinary message for all. Even brokers and agents in his area who see all this won't copycat it, because it's too much trouble. But then, nobody in his entire industry is ever going to see 300% to 1300% returns on marketing dollars, either.

One more example, from another GKIC Member, a chiropractor, Dr. Ken Vinton. Dr. Ken practices in a town of just 8,200 people. The month he provided me with the full-page newspaper ad shown to you in Figure 11.2, in pieces by necessity, on pages 119 and 120, he topped his best month in many years of practice, with over $70,000.00 in revenue, in large part thanks to this ad. What's important is that Ken is not running a traditional, broad 'n' sloppy, everything-chiropractic-done-here, for anybody 'n' everybody ad. Not at all. Instead, he is targeting, calling out to, and speaking to sufferers of chronic and severe pain who have tried medical treatment and OTC products unsuccessfully AND are being urged to go under the surgeon's knife. He has crafted a specific Message for a very specific prospective patient, with full knowledge that others will be quickly repelled by and disinterested in this ad.

So, you have a B2B and a consumer marketing example, demonstrating that the very same principles, strategies, and tactics apply in either sphere. Both these examples, in their own way, demonstrate "the Dale Carnegie Secret on Steroids." There is no reason you can't figure out and capitalize on this secret as well.

FIGURE 11.2: Dr. Ken Vinton Example

Reprinted from the *No B.S. Marketing Letter*, October 2012

FIGURE 11.2: Dr. Ken Vinton Example, cont.

Reprinted from the *No B.S. Marketing Letter,* October 2012

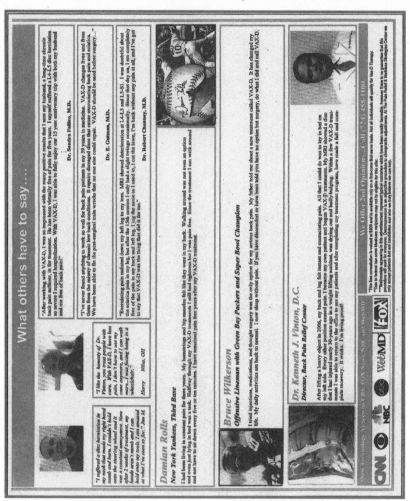

On a related note, I've done a monstrous amount of research, and gathered great actual examples, for books about two very specific demographic/psychographic target markets: one, boomers and seniors; the other, affluent consumers. Like a business niche that Gordon chooses to Message-Market Match to, or a group of severe back-pain sufferers flirting with last-resort surgery that Dr. Vinton addresses, these groups have their own tribal language, their own key interests, their own turn-ons and turn-offs.

The affluent and ultra-affluent market could be very important to you as a safer, higher ground in coming economic storms. My book, *No B.S. Guide to Marketing to the Affluent,* gives you complete guidance in appealing to and attracting more valuable customers, clients, or patients.

The boomer and senior market IS going to be important to you. By 2017, more than 50% of adult consumers in the U.S. will be over age 60, and they'll control 70% of discretionary spending. The Age/Profit Wave will determine the fate of almost every business, directly or indirectly. My newest book, *No B.S. Guide to Marketing to Leading-Edge Boomers and Seniors,* is your guide to winning with this consumer population.

Available at all fine booksellers.

Notes: These Examples—as well as all other Examples in this book—are copyright protected by their owners, used here with permission, but otherwise all rights reserved. Copying them in whole or large part, or their copy verbatim, is in violation of U.S. copyright law and can subject you to civil and criminal penalties. The examples in this chapter first appeared in my Million Dollar Marketing Lesson in *The No B.S. Marketing Letter* in October 2012. To receive the Letter every month, as part of a "test drive" by the author for readers of this book, see page 175.

APPLICATION

The following chapters from guest contributors provide an in-depth look at Direct Marketing applied.

One featured business is a law practice. This can serve as a model for anyone in any kind of professional practice, but it has broader application. In my book *No B.S. Guide to Trust-Based Marketing*, I make the case for and provide the methodology for positioning yourself as an expert authority and trusted advisor in any sort of business where services are offered and marketplace differentiation is critical. Ben Glass's Direct Marketing Law Practice is a good model for any business and businessperson seeking to advertise, market, promote, and sell with trusted-advisor positioning.

The other featured business is a real estate agent's. This is a more "approachable" and common consumer experience business than is a law practice. What works to attract homeowners and homebuyers can be translated to attract people to just about any service provider, retail outlet; by any sales professional, working with consumers or B2B.

In the Resources Section, organized by category of business, you'll find a list of other Direct Marketing leaders in varied fields and their websites, so that you can choose those most comparable to yours to study.

You can also obtain a voluminous, organized-by-category resource called The Magnetic System® rich with fill-in-the-blank templates as well as actual examples of advertising and marketing for every imagi nable purpose, for a full range of businesses converted to Direct Marketing Businesses at DanKennedy.com/Store.

CHAPTER 12

You Can Attract Your Ideal Customers, Clients, or Patients

Why Settle for Anything Else?

Ben Glass

What can a lawyer teach you about marketing? What I learned about marketing literally changed my life and could change yours. No, unless you are a lawyer, you weren't looking for a chapter here filled with law practice marketing examples. After all, what do we pesky lawyers know about marketing except to run lots of ads with gory accident scenes and fistfuls of dollars? I don't blame you for your revulsion. I share it. As you'll soon see, I found a road less traveled. My experience may fundamentally change the way you think about what you sell.

We'll start, though, back where I began, with traditional, commonplace legal advertising.

Drug or product reported killing or maiming people? Throw millions at it in TV and print ads "warning" consumers about the dangers and side effects and advising that "you may be entitled to compensation!"

If your traditional lawyer marketing doesn't work, get "creative" and have cartoons created showing yourself jumping over tall buildings or darting about in flying saucers.

Not dignified enough? Get "serious" and run ads showing the insurance companies "quaking" at the mere sound of your voice or mention of your name. Of course, you'd better be standing in front of those law books in your library when you create the ad!

Actually, if you are interested in marketing your professional practice, stick around and read this entire chapter. Here's why: There probably is not another professional services industry that spends, as a whole, as much on advertising as lawyers do. From websites to pay-per-click; from TV to radio, from print to billboards, lawyers hand over a ton of money to advertising reps, consultants, and to those selling the actual media. The competition among lawyers for new clients is enormous.

The legal profession is also the *second* most highly regulated professional services industry when it comes to advertising. (The financial planners have it worse, but there is not nearly as much money being spent to capture a new financial client as there is for law clients.)

In every town, there's the 800-pound gorilla that's outspending everyone else, too. You see his picture on every park bench, bus, and billboard. If there's a Yellow Pages directory still published in your town, his face together with an American flag likely adorns the back cover.

So if you are a lawyer, this chapter will help. If you are not a lawyer, this chapter will help even more because if I can help thousands of solo and small-firm lawyers compete against the 800-pound gorilla in their markets, and do so in an ethical, dignified way that helps many consumers get their problems solved, imagine what you can do in your industry where there is not nearly the level of money and sophistication being deployed by your competition.

If Lawyers Can Solve These Marketing Problems Then It's Gonna Be a Piece of Cake for You in Your Business

Here's the problems lawyers face when it comes to getting new clients:

1. There's a ton of us out there and many are willing and able to spend massive amounts of money on marketing.
2. There was no marketing class in law school, so we tend to just copy what other lawyers do, but do more of it.
3. Marketing is still, by and large, looked down upon by the established bar, and that segment of the bar tends to be the ones getting appointed to the committees that write the rules about advertising.
4. Most of what the public thinks they know about lawyers is derived from two sources: a) the silly "monkey-see, monkey-do" lawyer ads they do see, and b) massive anti-lawyer campaigns financed by insurance companies and big business. If someone has had an experience with an attorney, there is about a 50–50 chance that it was a negative experience because the "event" was the resolution of a dispute and the adversarial process is just no fun. This means that we have a huge "trust barrier" to overcome, as well.

Here's the Old Way Lawyers Solved the Problem of Breaking Through the Clutter

Here's the ad I ran when I first opened my own practice.

Look familiar? Of course it does. It's the same ad that nearly everyone runs in any business. It's the ad that says "I sure hope that by some random chance this ad provokes you to call me." Of course I copied the ad from someone else, but the Yellow Page rep selling me the ad said it was a "good one." She was the expert. What the heck did I know?

I was very proud of this ad and ran it for several years after I had left my old firm where I had worked for 12 years to start my own law practice in 1995.

Think it was a winner? Let me put it this way: The only people who called me from that ad were: 1) loser potential clients who had already been told "no" by all the other lawyers in the phone book, and 2) marketing vultures who saw me as an easy sell for their ads.

I struggled because while I had developed a successful track record as a young attorney and had won several important (and big) cases, there still was no good way for a potential client who might be looking for me to find me. Even if they found me there was no good way for me to differentiate myself in this very crowded and competitive marketplace. I couldn't think of a better way to say "Free Consultation" and "We Care."

Magnetic Marketing Changed My Life

Then one day in early 2003 I got a letter in the mail offering Dan Kennedy's "Magnetic Marketing" course. It was a long letter that promised that no matter what my business, I could market myself so that I would have a long line of people begging me to represent them. The letter hit on all of the problem spots that I outlined above. It talked about being seen as a commodity and constantly lowering my standards to service every person who called looking for a lawyer. I bit on the sales letter, and ordered Dan's program.

This was my introduction to Direct Marketing.

When the big box containing a huge three-ring binder and audio tapes (this was pre-CDs) arrived, I dove right in. I freely admit that after going through the tapes and the binder several times I still understood only about half of what Dan was talking about and I didn't even have a real good idea of exactly what "direct marketing" was, but I do distinctly remember thinking to myself that:

If I could figure out how to use what Dan and his Magnetic Marketing Course was talking about in my law practice, it would change everything.

I did figure it out.

Today, not only has my law practice (BenGlassLaw.com) boomed, I've created a huge information-marketing business (GreatLegalMarketing.com) that teaches lawyers in all different practice areas and in every part of the country how to more effectively market and build their practices. No more talking frogs and flying saucers for us!

Let me take you through the steps that we now use to market BenGlassLaw (BenGlassLaw.com). Our small firm now has 13 branch offices throughout much of Virginia. All of the growth is driven by direct-response marketing. It's the only marketing we do. Clients come to me "pre-sold." They often speak of already "knowing me" from reading my books, watching my DVDs, and viewing many online videos.

Your job, when you get through this chapter and the rest of this book, is to figure out how you can use what's here to market your business. You need to be smart enough to translate "client" to "patient" or "customer."

Five Secrets to Using Direct-Response Marketing to Market Your Professional Practice

1. Identify your "perfect client" before you do anything.
2. No matter how much or how little the prospect knows about you or your services, create irresistible offers that literally compel them to say: "Market to me more."
3. Don't buy more ads—instead, get "in front of" your competition.
4. Embrace the complexity of marketing and work hard to develop marketing that talks to your best prospects no matter where they are on the "moving parade of interest."
5. Develop a follow-up system, because the real treasure is buried there.

Secret #1: Identify Your "Perfect Client" Before You Start to Market

If you have clients right now in your office who are making your life miserable, you have only yourself to blame! Your marketing attracted them and your fear that you'd never get another client let them in the door when they came a-knocking!

You must start by clearly identifying who you want to see walking through that door. My friend Matt Zagula, co-author with Dan of *No B.S. Trust-Based Marketing,* calls his perfect client in the financial services industry his "avatar client." Both Matt and I have "drawn" the image of our favorite type of client in our minds, put that image on paper, and have created marketing that is specifically designed to attract only that type of client.

Remember, I'm a personal injury lawyer. You might say "Ben, how could there be a 'profile' of a 'perfect' personal injury client?" After all, car hits car, it's pretty random, isn't it? Don't personal injury lawyers want to represent everybody?

Lawyers who don't know anything about marketing do say they want to represent "everybody," but that's only because they don't know any better. They are also the ones first to complain about all the undesirable clients whose files bark at them from the file cabinet.

My perfect client is someone who is middle to upper class; educated; has plenty of car and health insurance; is looking for a respected authority (and not just a lottery payout) from whom they will take advice. Of course, we are also looking for large damages cases and we are not shy about saying that. My marketing is designed to attract that client and to repel anyone who doesn't match that model.

For a little bit of "inside baseball," here's a list of attributes that I don't want to see in a client:

- Thinks their injury is the path to riches
- Claims that it's the "principle that matters" and they aren't really "interested in the money"
- Is on their third lawyer for this case and first wants to talk about "how their other two lawyers screwed up a great case"

- Wants to instruct me on the law and the value of their case
- Wants to make sure the defendant pays with their own blood (in addition to any insurance money)
- Has had multiple accidents and a history of pain in the same area where pain is claimed now
- Claims a large injury but bumper on car shows only a scratch
- Wants to collect for lost wages but hasn't paid taxes in years

My "perfect" may not be your "perfect," but you need to know who your "perfect" is or you'll be back to attracting everyone with your "free consultation" or lowest-price marketing.

Secret #2: Create Offers That Compel Them to Beg for <u>More</u> Marketing Messages from You

No matter how much or how little the prospect knows about you or your services, you must never again develop any marketing piece that doesn't invite your prospect to contact you to request even more information from you.

The very best marketers in any industry do not have just one information offer for each product/service. They have multiple offers, each masterfully created with this thought in mind: The potential client may know nothing about what I am selling; they may know "A" but not "B"; they may have already researched the product/service a lot or they may be seeing me at the beginning of their research.

As we will see, prospective clients go through a multistep decision-making process. You never know, because *they* (not you) control when and where they enter your world, what they've seen, heard about, or believe before they notice you for the first time. Were you having this discussion with them "live" in their living room or your office, this would be easy. You could gauge where they are in the buying process and adjust your presentation accordingly.

The key is to offer something of real value to them right up front. We do it with a number of free books they can download and videos they can watch. This starts to build trust but also tells them that there is "more behind the door" and all they have to do is ask for it.

Secret #3: It's a Fool's Game to Try to Simply Outspend Your Competition—You Need to Get in Front of the Crowd of Competitors by Shouting a Different Message

Most lawyers wait until someone has already made the decision to hire an attorney before they begin to market to them. That's why most lawyer ads are all about the experience or "caring attitude" or reputation of the lawyer.

Thinking of nothing better than "**Dewy Cheatum and Howe, We Care for You and Offer Free Consultations**," most lawyers then try to beat the competition by simply buying more ads. This is risky, expensive, and dumb.

First, waiting until someone has decided to find a lawyer is too late. You can actually begin to market to potential clients (and get them to listen to you) before they have reached that point. We do it with this message:

If you have been injured in an accident you may not need an attorney. But, before you 1) talk to the insurance adjuster, 2) hire an attorney, or 3) sign any forms, contact us, and get our free consumer guides.

With our free information you will learn 1) How to avoid the five major mistakes that new accident

victims make with an insurance adjuster, and 2) how to find the right lawyer for your case.

You see, we know what is running through our prospect's mind just after an accident. For example, they want to know a couple of things shortly after they've been in an accident:

1. Should I talk to the insurance adjuster who keeps calling and give the recorded statement he keeps bugging me about?
2. Should I sign the insurance forms they keep sending over? What about accident-related forms my own insurance company wants me to sign?
3. Can I handle this on my own or do I need to hire an attorney right away?
4. Which insurance company will pay my mounting doctor bills?

Our initial messaging says to a consumer: Wait, slow down, don't panic. We can help you BEFORE you decide if you even need an attorney or not. That's what I mean by "getting in front of the crowd."

Secret #4: Embrace the Complexity of Good Marketing and Work Hard to Develop Marketing That Talks to Your Best Prospects No Matter Where They Are on the "Moving Parade of Interest"

The "moving parade of interest" is a term I first learned from Dan Kennedy. It means that your prospects go through a process when making a hiring decision. The problem for you is that you can't control where they are along that "moving parade" when they first notice you.

Think of it this way. The last time you bought a new car, you likely didn't just wake up one day and say 1) I want a new car, *and* 2) it's going to be a Lexus, *and* 3) it's going to be silver *and* 4) it's got to have a premium sound system.

Unless your old car was totaled in an accident, you went on a "decision path" that likely went something like this:

1. My old car is looking a bit dull.
2. I deserve a new car.
3. I can afford the new car I deserve.
4. I like the following brands: Lexus, BMW, Ford.
5. OK, I really like the Lexus.
6. Wow, there's all these Lexus ads on TV.
7. Let's visit the Lexus website where I can "design my own car."
8. Let's go for a test drive.
9. OK, I've decided I want the RX 350.
10. Let's see where in town I can get the best deal on the silver RX 350 with premium sound.

If a car dealer is doing a good job with their marketing, they are going to develop messages and marketing materials (DVDs, online videos, testimonials) that address you no matter where you are and push you to the next level until you convince yourself that the silver Lexus RX 350 must have been built with just you in mind!

This is where it gets complex. (*Mindset note*: Embrace the complexity. Your competition is lazy. Do this work.) You need to create marketing messages that speak to your prospects wherever they are. Here are some examples in my world:

- In an accident and have literally no clue as to what to do next. (Free download of my book at www.The AccidentBook.com)
- Have some clue about what to do but want to try to settle the case themselves. (Free download: www. GetItSettled.com)

- Have learned that trying to settle a claim themselves is more complicated than they thought and want to hire an attorney but don't have a clue as to how to choose one lawyer over another. (Free download: www.TheTruthAboutLawyerAds.com)
- Like everything they see about us, but made the mistake of hiring another lawyer before they saw us and want to fire that lawyer. (www.FireMyAttorney.com)
- Had a case before but didn't get as much money as they could have because they bought the wrong type or amount of car insurance. (Free download: www. TheInsuranceBook.com)
- Have a very specific question about some small part of the whole claims process? (We've probably answered it at www.LegalAcademyVideos.com.)

Those are the steps for grabbing a person's interest no matter where they are on the "moving parade of interest." Remember, though, you *must* create marketing like this for each of your practice areas. The questions and concerns that a divorce client has are different from someone who was arrested last night and different from the guy who was in a car accident. One size does NOT fit all.

Yes, it took a lot of work to produce all that content, and I haven't even shown you the follow-up that "backs up" each point of entry. Embrace it!

Secret #5: Develop a Follow-Up System Because the Real Treasure Is Buried There

All we have really done so far is to get the attention of someone who may be a prospect for you. No matter where they were in their thinking when they discovered your message, you've now had them identify themselves to you and you have been given some level of permission to market to them.

This is huge! Congratulate yourself.

Now we reel them in with a comprehensive follow-up campaign that provides overwhelming proof that you are the wise man at the top of the mountain.

"Oh Ben, more work! Are you crazy?"

Nope. Here's what we know not only from my own practice but from the feedback we get from thousands of lawyers who listen to me in every type of practice area and in every type of market: an extensive, multistep multimedia marketing campaign directed to someone who is now paying attention to you is the Holy Grail of marketing.

Don't wimp out now!

No matter where along the "moving parade of interest" a prospect is when they first ask for information, they are going to get one of our free instant downloads and an invitation to get "more" for a trade of full contact information from them.

When they give us full contact information and enough evidence that they've actually been in a car accident in Virginia, then they are going to get our "Ben Glass Law Shock and Awe Package." We tell them to be on the lookout for it. This big envelope contains a number of our books, a TV interview on DVD, a radio interview on CD, and number of other free reports that that will be helpful to them.

We follow this up with more mailed packages, books with more books, and free reports. Of course there is also a series of auto-responder emails. The content of the emails differ depending on whether the prospect has told us that they are "just curious about what we are doing" (as you may indicate when you go to any of the URLs in this chapter and request information) or whether they have provided us with enough proof that they just might be a good prospect for us.

Warning: Do not make the mistake of relying on auto-responder emails only! Nothing beats the mailman bringing a package to the prospect's house. Our marketing system is run with Infusionsoft. Frankly, we've found nothing better and have been a raving fan for over six years. (You can learn more at www.infusionsoft.com.)

Let me leave you with this fact from our own experience in switching all of our marketing in the law firm to direct-response marketing (Kennedy-style):

> We discovered that our best clients hire us anywhere from 3 to 12 months *after* first entering one of our direct-response marketing funnels. Our perfect client is taking the time to 1) heal from serious injuries and 2) do research before making the decision as to which lawyer to hire, and when they show up in our office they are 3) usually carrying with them the big bundle of stuff we've sent them. Importantly, we are making more money and having more fun.

Now it's your turn. If my profession can do it, you've got no excuse.

Ben Glass is a practicing personal injury and medical malpractice attorney in Virginia. He is also the founder of Great Legal Marketing, and the author of *Great Legal Marketing* and *How Smart Lawyers Think, Behave and Market to Get More Clients, Make More Money and Still Get Home in Time for Dinner* (www.GreatLegalMarketingBook.com). Ben can be found at: www.BenGlassLaw.com or www.GreatLegalMarketing.com.

CHAPTER 13

They All Laughed When I Stopped Selling My Products—
Until I Became a Top Agent and Transformed My Entire Industry

Craig Proctor

I f you're a serious student of direct-response headlines, you recognize the famous headline reworked as my chapter title. It's accurate, because just about every real estate agent and broker I knew when I literally stopped advertising and marketing myself and my properties *laughed*. When I started making the radical changes described in this chapter, I was all alone.

My story is about my real estate career, but I promise, there are eight breakthrough strategies here that can radically reinvent almost any business for the better.

I became the top REMAX® agent in the world at age 29. For 22 years, I averaged selling a home every day! Along the way, other agents stopped laughing and started asking how I was achieving such extraordinary success. I've trained and coached over 30,000 agents, and no less than Michael Gerber, author of the best-selling book on systems in business, *The E-Myth,* characterized me as "a visionary who reinvented the job called real estate and teaches agents about freedom rather than about work." I'm the guy who brought Direct-Response Advertising to real estate. I'm famous enough as a leader in the field that, in recent years, I've been copycatted and had my material taken and taught by quite a few people. I'm still innovating, though, so hundreds of agents who've been in my coaching programs for years continue and hundreds more join month by month.

This lofty perch seemed unimaginable when I began my real estate career. When I started out, I made the same fundamental mistake 99% of all beginners make—and many keep making forever: I looked around at how everybody else was doing it and simply copied them, striving to excel by out-working my competitors. This turned into a demoralizing period in my life. I spent my days and nights cold-calling, door-knocking, doing floor time at the office, wasting weekends at open houses. I soon hated going to work, to face rejection after rejection. Most importantly, my real estate business wasn't working for me financially.

Eventually I got so sick and tired of nauseating and highly inefficient prospecting that I decided there had to be a better way, and, like many before me, I decided that this better way had to be advertising. Once I began advertising, I reasoned, my troubles would be over. Instead of me chasing prospects, prospects would now come flocking to me!

Well, that's not exactly what happened. Again, my strategy was to copy what those around me were doing. This led to very traditional ads—a big picture of me and a catchy slogan. You see ads like this every day in your own real estate publications, and you might ask yourself, "What's so wrong with these ads?" The problem with self-image advertising is that the focus is on the "agent" when it really should be on the "customer."

My first ads may have drawn attention to me (see an awful example of my early advertising in Figure 13.1), but they didn't get me business because they didn't offer prospects

FIGURE 13.1: Great Example of a Bad Ad

OUTSTANDING in his field

Don't take chances. List with #1

CRAIG PROCTOR

898-1211

Omega Realty (1988) Ltd.,
1140 Stellar Drive, Newmarket, Ontario L3Y 7B7

A great example of a really bad ad I ran early in my career.

anything they cared about—there were no customer benefits or reasons for a prospect to contact me. Whether you know it or not, your prospects are all tuned to the same radio station: WIFM (What's in it for me). If your ad can't answer this question, chances are your prospects won't bother to even look at your ad, let alone respond to it. Lesson learned. I found out the hard and expensive way that just because prospects know who you are doesn't mean they'll call you.

I needed to find a solution. The problem was, while prospecting bled me emotionally, image advertising bled me financially. I didn't know how to make this business work for me and I actually considered getting out of real estate, but since I had nowhere else to go, I was driven to figure it out. This was 1989 and I had just heard through a friend about a "marketing renegade" with a refreshing, but unorthodox approach to advertising. His name was Dan Kennedy, and I still remember seeing the picture of him sitting on a bull. How appropriate, given this guy was positioned as "no B.S."

Dan introduced me to the concept of Direct-Response Advertising: the premise that every ad must be held accountable to garner an immediate and direct response; that every penny I spent on advertising must be trackable and therefore testable; that what was missing in 99.9% of marketing campaigns was strategy.

As you'll see shortly, I aggressively applied this principle to all of my marketing, and the payoff for me was huge. What I realized is that not only were the ads that most agents placed ineffective, the strategic foundation of the entire industry was all wrong. There are really only two things that most real estate agents advertise: *themselves* and *houses*. I was no different, until I took a step back and analyzed what I really wanted my advertising to do to get prospects to call me. While that may sound self-evident, when I evaluated traditional industry ads against this mandate, I realized that they not only fell short, they actually did a much better job of *repelling* prospects than *attracting* them.

Breakthrough #1: The One Reason

My industry's mistakes with advertising are not at all unique. In fact, the majority of all advertising is about the advertiser or the product. My solutions also apply to many other kinds of businesses. The radical change I made—at the time, ahead of anyone else in my field—is one you can profit from as well.

The radical premise I committed to was and is: <u>The only reason</u> to advertise is to get prospects to call you.

Let's reject Image Advertising first. Even if you're not a real estate agent, you have most certainly seen these self-promotional ads where the agent paying for the ad talks about how great they are, their designations, how honest and hardworking they are, etc. Let me be clear about the fact that no one cares. Despite this, year in and year out, in every marketplace across the country, real estate agents waste vast sums of money on beautiful pictures of themselves with catchy slogans that no one pays attention to.

Breakthrough #2: Replace Image Ads with USP Ads

In stark contrast to ineffective Image Advertising, Dan introduced me to the concept of Unique Selling Proposition (USP), challenging me to answer for my real estate business the most important question on every prospect's mind, i.e., "Why should I do business with you versus all other options, including doing nothing at all?" This made total sense to me and I jumped all over it. I started to test different USP messages and quickly came up with a winner, which I aggressively used: "Your Home Sold in 120 Days or I'll Buy It." This very effectively positioned me as "the guy who'll buy your home if it doesn't sell" and this irresistible consumer benefit drove truckloads of business to my door like never before. I never looked back.

In a slowing Toronto real estate market in the early 1990s, my Guaranteed Home Sale Program helped me succeed because it solved a very important consumer problem. While every agent will promise to sell your home, I guaranteed it—a very meaningful and compelling consumer benefit (see Figure 13.2). In fact, several times a day the phone would ring with prospects asking: "How does this 'you'll buy my home thing' work?" to which I would reply: "I need to see your home before I can tell you how much I will buy it for." This of course made perfect sense to sellers, and now I was face-to-face with

FIGURE 13.2: Marketing USP

A rider on all my signs marketed my powerful USP.

someone who wanted to sell their home . . . always a good thing if you're a real estate agent.

Now, I know what you're thinking—how the heck did I buy all of those homes? The truth is that during my entire 22-year real estate career I only bought two homes, and that occurred when I broke my own rules. Over the past 20 years, I have been responsible for bringing the Guaranteed Sale Program mainstream by introducing the rules and conditions of this program to thousands of real estate agents in my seminars and coaching programs. You can get more information on the GSP and everything else I teach, including free training, at **www. NoBSRealEstateMarketing.com.** *(WARNING: Other seminar/ training organizations have tried to copy what I created but don't really understand the inner workings of the GSP.)*

I have already discussed why Image Advertising is completely inefficient. By simply replacing my image ads with USP ads, I got an immediate and dramatic increase in sales. With USP advertising, I not only created massive awareness in my marketplace, I also successfully attached a very powerful and tangible consumer benefit to my identity, so not only did prospects know who I was, they also understood exactly what made me different and better than my competition, and they had a specific reason to call me.

This is the heart and soul of Direct-Response Advertising: a specific reason to respond to you.

The GSP is only one of the many successful strategies I teach real estate agents, but because it's *perceived* to be risky, this is NOT where I begin with agents who are new to *"The Craig Proctor Real Estate Success System."*

I said there were two things that real estate agents traditionally advertise. The second is their property listings (products). In fact, millions of dollars are wasted every single day on this very ineffective strategy that most agents would agree nets them few results, certainly not enough to pay for the ads.

You may ask why agents keep doing this if it doesn't really work. Well, there are three reasons:

1. Every other agent does it this way, so it seems like the right thing to do.
2. Agents don't have a better strategy to attract buyers.
3. Sellers demand it because other agents keep doing it, and on and on it goes.

None of those seemed like very good reasons to me, so I focused on discovering a better and more effective strategy. The solution I discovered to both better promote my listings and attract buyers changed my business virtually overnight. My secret formula is incredibly simple, and here it is:

Breakthrough #3: The Most Effective and Least Expensive Way to Generate Leads Is to Offer Prospects Something They Want and Make It Easy and Non-Threatening for Them to Get It

As soon as I understood the power of this simple principle, all my marketing has been built around it. In every single ad and marketing communication I invest in, I make the offer so appealing and so easy to get that the right prospects unfailingly respond by contacting me to do business. This is the essence of Direct-Response Marketing. It is marketing that causes your prospects to immediately act—to respond to you directly because they really want what you're offering. Remember, "the only reason to run an ad is to get prospects to contact you."

Pick up the classified section of your local paper, or browse Craigslist online under "Homes for Sale" to see what

I mean. I want to make a very important point that I believe will shock many of you. The fact of the matter is, the role of a property classified ad, whether in print or online, is NOT to sell the property in the ad.

I'll go further than that and state: "It is virtually IMPOSSIBLE to sell a house with a classified ad." What happens MOST often is that a buyer calls about a listing, and as the agent begins to describe the property to them, the buyer begins to eliminate it and politely tells the agent that it's either too big or too small, in the wrong area, too much money, or whatever, and hangs up the phone. When I explain it in this way, agents can see that the ad doesn't often sell the house they are advertising. So if it's next to impossible to sell the house in the ad, why do agents keep trying to do so by babbling on and on with lengthy descriptions of property features?

When agents are writing their classified ads, they shouldn't be thinking about how to showcase all the wonderful features of this house, instead they should be thinking about how they can get the highest response.

So what are the benefits that will be most motivating to prospects?

When you scan the classified section of almost any paper, you see that agents fill their ads with unemotional property features: walk-in closets, new roof, central vacuum, etc., instead of using words that actually strike an emotional chord with buyers.

Let's take a look at two ad examples in Figure 13.3, which describe the exact same property. I think you'll agree that the property ad on the top is very typical of the kind of ads most agents run.

Staying for a moment with this typical agent ad, let's talk about the process of elimination. Agents inadvertently penalize themselves by adding eliminating words to their ads

FIGURE 13.3

> NARROW FUNNEL:
> EXAMPLE OF A TYPICAL
> "FEATURE-DRIVEN" AD
> (DON'T DO THIS!)
>
> NEWMARKET—2 bdrm, corner lot, closet organizers, garage door openers, water softener, new dishwasher, $279,900. Call (905)830-1234. Bob Smith, XYZ Realty.
>
> WIDE FUNNEL:
> EXAMPLE OF A GREAT
> "EMOTIONAL-BENEFIT"
> DIRECT-RESPONSE AD
>
> NEWMARKET—Lovely Homes, quiet streets, great neighborhood. Free list with pics at www.NewmarketHomesList.com
> Free recorded message 1-800-000-0000 ID#0000

that actually cause prospects NOT to respond. For example, the ad on the top advertises that the house is a two-bedroom, and there are many great prospects who will immediately eliminate this house as they feel it's too small. The same thing applies to "corner lot." Some prospects like a corner lot, but some don't. The ones who don't will eliminate the ad. Elimination means they won't call the agent, which means the agent never gets a chance to tell them about different listings they would be interested in, and thus they never have a chance to convert the buyer to a client. So as you can see, by focusing on the specific, unemotional features of a property, agents vastly limit the number of good prospects who will respond to their ad.

Breakthrough #4: Instead of Advertising What You "Have," Call Out to Your Prospects by Advertising What They "Want"

Let's look at the ad on the bottom to help you understand the big innovation I brought to this industry. I've helped agents make more money by <u>NOT</u> advertising their listings.

My method stops agents from advertising "what they have"—i.e., their listings. What I've taught agents to do instead is to craft ads that call out to who they most want to attract. With this strategy, I teach agents to write ads that focus on who they want to attract instead of trying to sell the listing they have.

The fact is that agents are not enslaved to only sell their own listings. They can sell a buyer anything on MLS. So, instead of focusing their advertising on offering prospects only what they "have"—i.e., their listings—I've taught agents to offer what it is that prospects "want," and there's no rule that says the properties they offer have to be their own listings. More than anything else, what today's real estate consumers want is variety, choice, great deals, hard-to-find properties, AND they want accessing this information to be easy and non-threatening. So I teach agents to give them exactly that. After all, it's very difficult to eliminate an entire list of homes.

Breakthrough #5: People Do NOT Want to Be Sold

Another very important thing I want you to notice about the ad on the bottom is that the call to action does NOT direct prospects to call "me." I teach agents to provide prospects a non-threatening way to get the information they offer by driving prospects to a website and/or toll-free recorded hotline, both of which offer prospects the information they want in exchange for their contact info. I call these my automated robots, because they automatically handle all prospect inquiries for me. The result? Now I have good quality leads to follow up with because the very nature of the information I offer (such as a list of homes) is only of interest to real prospects.

Most businesses have an opportunity to use this very same strategy—and it can change everything.

There are several important advantages to driving prospect inquiries to automated robots such as a hotline or a website. From a marketing perspective, it has been proven that three times as many prospects will respond if they don't have to speak with a salesperson to get the information they're after. Why? Because people do NOT want to be sold. If you make a great offer but tell people they have to call a salesperson directly to get it, you'll significantly lower your response. Also, these robots give you the important ability to scientifically track every ad you run.

In addition to these marketing advantages, there's a huge lifestyle advantage to driving prospects to a website and/ or hotline—one that will change your whole way of doing business. You see, with this strategy, the prospect is not actually calling the agent directly. Instead, they're calling to get the information offered in the ad, so prospects are not even expecting a call back from the agent. It *is* important that agents follow up with prospects so they can convert inquiries into a face-to-face appointment, but now—instead of the agent being interrupted with prospect inquiries 24/7—they simply call the prospect back when it's convenient for them.

Breakthrough #6: Replace Your Property (Product) Ads with My Wide-Funnel Ads That Offer Lists of Homes Your Prospects Cannot Eliminate

Imagine generating so much business that you can effectively raise the bar and ONLY work with the most sincere, most motivated, most ready-to-act prospects, prospects that will work with you and not fight you. Using the simple, inexpensive little ads I developed, my students have been able to do exactly this. By using my ads to generate dozens of qualified leads week in and week out, they now have the luxury of choice and can pick and choose who they want to work with. They can set their own rules of engagement and do business on <u>their</u> terms.

Breakthrough #7: Increase Demand by Creating Competition and Urgency

Another innovation I'm known for is my re-invention of the traditional open house. The Old School approach has the agent open a home for three to four hours on Saturday and Sunday afternoons hoping and praying that a buyer will walk in the door and say, "WOW, this is the home of my dreams," and then buy it. I'm not saying that this never happens, but it's a very low probability game (less than 1% of homes are ever sold in this way). In fact, if it happens, the agent just got rewarded for bad behavior and may be convinced to continue with this inefficient approach.

Early in my career I wasted many weekends doing this exact thing. Sitting alone in a stranger's home does give one plenty of time to think, and what I sat and thought about was the same thing all entrepreneurs think about in times of crisis: "There must be a better way." So on one of those Sunday afternoons all those years ago as I sat at an open house, I was thinking about something my father had recently shared with me. My father has many rental properties, and one night at dinner he shared his frustration of agreeing to meet with a prospective tenant, only to be stood up. Sick and tired of all the time he wasted on these no-shows, he finally said "no more" and changed his approach. Instead of meeting tenants individually, he decided to force all of the tenants to meet him at the rental property at the exact same time. Under this new scenario, he no longer cared if some of the prospects didn't show. As an added bonus, the many that did show were now competing for the one and only rental opportunity. My dad no longer had to sell the virtues of the rental property because tenants were literally throwing their deposits on the table.

I got to thinking that this same strategy just might work for me. So the next weekend, instead of opening one home, I decided to open six of my listings on the same afternoon and the "Craig Proctor Sunday Tour of Homes" was born. I purposely forced all of the buyers to each home at the same time. Each home was open for exactly 10 minutes with 15 minutes of travel time between homes. So the first home was open from 1:00 to 1:10 pm, the next home from 1:25 to 1:35, etc. I was able to conduct the entire event on my own because I could get from house to house in 15 minutes. Halfway through my very first Tour of Homes I knew this was a game-changer. Not only did many buyers show up at each home, but each buyer saw other buyers who also appeared interested and an "auction effect" was created. No more selling. My properties sold for more money in less time, buyers loved it, and for the next 18 years I never conducted a traditional open house again.

Breakthrough #8: Always Find Innovative Ways to Get Prospects Hunting You Rather Than You Chasing Them

Much of my success is the result of challenging and vastly improving on the traditional way things were done in my industry. This became a way of thinking for me and I want to share three more examples with you.

The Reverse Offer

This strategy helps agents get their seller's home sold in a buyer's market. Traditionally, buyers view many listings before making an offer on a home. What that means, of course, is that only one seller is going to get the offer.

This is a very passive approach, and one in which the seller's odds of being the loser are much higher than their odds of winning. As a Plan B, what I teach agents to do is make a reverse offer, and here's how it works. When we list a property, we have the seller sign a purchase and sale agreement, complete with a good price, flexible terms, and a cover letter (which we call a Love Letter) from the seller. The Love Letter describes why the home is right for the buyers— the schools, the community, the church, and the neighbors—all positive. This offer is then packaged and when a prospective buyer previews the home and is not forthcoming with an offer within 48 hours, my seller makes a reverse offer to the buyer. The offer gets sent over to the buyer's agent and presented as any offer would with a 48-hour expiration.

The worst-case scenario is that the buyer says no thanks, but often what happens is that the buyer says, "Well, I would buy the property at 'x' . . .". The seller now knows the buyer's "x" and can respond accordingly. In essence, the buyers counteroffer. You would be amazed at the number of buyers who are on the fence regarding one house or another. The problem is that they have the universe to choose from due to the high levels of homes for sale. A little nudge or "reverse offer" from the seller can often help them see through the overwhelming supply and develop a top-of-mind awareness of the seller's home.

Paying the Long-Distance Bill

As you can imagine, I sold a lot of real estate in my marketplace, a bedroom community called Newmarket, 30 minutes north of Toronto, Ontario. I wanted to find a way to give back to my community while at the same time promoting myself. Traditionally, agents have done this by handing out notepads, pumpkin seeds, or calendars with their name on them. Most of this stuff ends up at the bottom of a drawer or in the garbage—another waste of an agent's money. I decided to do something different. At the time, a disadvantage of living in Newmarket was that residents had to dial long distance to call Toronto, something the average resident had to do a lot, at great expense (this was before all the cheap, North American-wide long-distance plans). So I promoted a special Toll-Free line (939-FREE) that enabled residents to call Toronto for free after listening to a ten-second message from me (I recorded several messages promoting my USPs, which rotated). This simple idea not only created massive good will and awareness, it also generated huge PR for me, both locally and nationally (I was featured in national newspapers and on national TV news shows like *CBC Venture*).

Over-the-Phone Homeseller Seminar

Traditionally, agents conduct buyer and seller seminars at their offices or at a local hotel as a way of selling to many prospects at the same time. But remember Breakthrough #5—People Do NOT Want to be Sold. What I did instead was offer an over-the-phone homeseller seminar as an easy and non-threatening way to get my prospects to raise their hands. My ad for the over-the-phone seminar was designed to look like a public service announcement, and I asked a real estate lawyer and mortgage broker to join me to host the call. While callers were not asked to identify themselves in order to participate, each of the panelists offered a free report with valuable information that the most qualified seller prospects would crave. Of course, in order for prospects to receive these reports, they had to leave their contact information, providing me a great lead to follow up with.

Real estate done the traditional way is frequently difficult, unprofitable, and unrewarding for agents. No wonder 82% don't make it to their fifth anniversary and why there's such burn and churn in the industry. Agents who learn my system have an entirely different experience. They make much more money in far less time, giving them more freedom to do the things they really want to do.

If my innovative approach to this business intrigues you, there are many easy entry points to my system, which you'll see when you visit www.NoBSRealEstateMarketing.com, but one of the simplest ways to get involved is to sign up for my FREE training programs and information that will allow you to test my system in your business and even benefit from live weekly training that will show you how to get started with my system. If you can copy, you can succeed. My system has been responsible for the biggest success stories in the industry, with thousands of my members earning high six- and seven-figure incomes as a result of what they've learned from me. These are the top agents in the country. You could be next.

If you are not a real estate agent, I hope you'll think about my experiences and breakthroughs as a fill-in-the-blank challenge for your business. Push yourself to find an application of each of my eight breakthroughs. Just as I figured these out for myself to radically reinvent the real estate business, you can for your business, too.

Known within the industry as the King of Lead Generation, Craig Proctor (the top agent for RE/MAX® Worldwide for several years) not only sold over $1 billion of real estate himself in his 20+ year career, but he's also coached more agents to millionaire status than any other coach or trainer. While the cornerstone of Craig's system is lead generation using his famous "Reverse Prospecting," Craig's is a comprehensive system, which also includes highly effective scripts, conversion, and presentation systems, to empower agents to follow their leads through to maximum profit. By openly sharing his step-by-step approach, Craig Proctor has trained over 30,000 agents worldwide on how to create a business that serves their lives providing them more money, more time, and more freedom.

RESOURCES

Direct Marketing
Businesses to Study

Retail

Gardner's Mattress & More
www.GardnersMattressAndMore.com

SunYourBuns
www.sunyourbuns.com

Iron Tribe Fitness
www.irontribefitness.com

Columbia Arts Academy
www.columbiaartsacademy.com

Imperial Auto Castle
ImperialAutoCastle.com

Restaurants

Diana's Gourmet Pizzeria
www.dianasgourmetpizzeria.ca

Professional Practices

Dr. Greg Nielsen, DC
www.docnielsen.com

Dr. Charles Martin DDS
www.MasterYourPractice.com

Ben Glass—Ben Glass Law
www.BenGlassLaw.com

Steinbacher & Stahl, Elder Law
www.sselderlaw.com

Sales Professionals

Walter Bergeron (Industrial)
www.powercontrolservices.com

Gordon Quinton
www.SepticInsurance.com
www.PavingInsurance.com
www.NoHassleRestaurant Insurance.com

Miscellaneous

Amy Barnhardt
www.StrongMarriageNow.com

Ron Wolforth—Pitching Central
www.PitchingCentral.com

John DuCane
www.DragonDoor.com

Darin Spindler
www.KidsBowlFree.com

Paul Baeppler—P.I.
www.integrityohio.com

About the Author

Dan S. Kennedy is a multimillionaire serial entrepreneur, strategic advisor, and marketing consultant, and one of the highest paid direct-response advertising copywriters in America. He has been a celebrated thought leader in the field of marketing for more than three decades. He has been intimately involved in epic marketing success stories involving virtually every media including print, direct mail, direct-response radio and TV, TV infomercials, and online media. Dan routinely engineers million-dollar to multimillion-dollar improvements to clients' marketing campaigns, multimillion-dollar product launches, and brokered joint ventures and strategic alliances that yield new opportunities. He has assisted one of the fastest growth franchisors of recent history; a company grown from startup to nearly $2 billion by direct marketing; one of the fastest growing small-business software companies; and networks of restaurants, service businesses, health-care practices, and financial advisory practices numbering in the thousands. All told, he influences more than 1 million small-business owners and entrepreneurs annually through these networks and through his newsletters.

To communicate with Mr. Kennedy directly about his availability for speaking engagements and development and presentation of customized speeches, seminars, or corporate training programs; availability of mastermind meetings; consulting, copywriting, or co-authorship, please fax your inquiry to (602) 269-3113, write to Kennedy Inner Circle, Inc. at 15433 N. Tatum Blvd. #104, Phoenix, Arizona 85032, or phone (602) 997-7707. Mr. Kennedy famously does not use email or other online communication.

For information about his books, newsletters, resources published by GKIC, and GKIC conferences: www.NoBSBooks. com and www.DanKennedy.com.

Other Books by the Author

In the No B.S. series, published by Entrepreneur Press

No B.S. Guide to Marketing to Leading-Edge Boomers and Seniors (with Chip Kessler)

No B.S. Guide to Trust-Based Marketing (with Matt Zagula)

No B.S. Price Strategy (with Jason Marrs)

No B.S. Guide to Marketing to the Affluent

No B.S. Business Success in the New Economy

No B.S. Sales Success in the New Economy

No B.S. Wealth Attraction in the New Economy

No B.S. Guide to Ruthless Management of People and Profits

No B.S. Time Management for Entrepreneurs

Other Books by Dan Kennedy

Ultimate Marketing Plan (4th Edition—20th Anniversary Edition), Adams Media

Ultimate Sales Letter (4th Edition—20th Anniversary Edition), Adams Media

The New Psycho-Cybernetics with Dr. Maxwell Maltz (Prentice-Hall)

Unfinished Business/Autobiographical Essays, Advantage

Making Them Believe: The 21 Principles and Lost Secrets of Dr. Brinkley-Style Marketing with Chip Kessler, GKIC/Morgan-James

Make 'Em Laugh & Take Their Money, GKIC/Morgan-James

Other Books

Uncensored Sales Strategies by Sydney Barrows (with Dan Kennedy), Entrepreneur Press

Index

THE **MOST**
INCREDIBLE
Free Gift **EVER**

Learn How to claim your $633.91 Worth of Pure,
Powerful Money-Making Information Absolutely FREE

Including a FREE "Test-Drive" of
GKIC Insider's Circle Gold Membership

All You Have To Do is Go Here Now:
DANKENNEDY.COM/BUSINESSES